BITCOIN 101

•────────•

Mastering the Future of Money in Just 21 Days

2nd Edition : Feb 2025

This Book is Dedicated to my Mom and Dad for unwavering love and support - Guma Dahal │ Kaladhar Dahal

-Krishna Dahal

© Krishna Dahal 2025

Supporters for the Book

Dipti Gyawali   Prashant Soni   Bibek Kunwar   Sharmila Rijal

Salina Paudel   Sagar Chaudhary   Saroj Bhandari   Priyanka Bhandari

Subash Pandey   Megh Raj Kandel

Table of Contents

Preface

Chapter 1: Magic of Money — 1

Chapter 2: Finding Satoshi Nakamoto — 11

Chapter 3: Capping the World at 21 Million — 18

Chapter 4: Halving Supply Shock — 25

Chapter 5: Proof of Work vs Out of Thin Air — 31

Chapter 6: Becoming a Node. Verify, Don't Trust — 39

Chapter 7: Civil War of 2017 — 47

Chapter 8: Break Me (Bitcoin) if You Can — 55

Chapter 9: Scaling Into the Future — 62

Chapter 10: How to Acquire Bitcoin — 70

Chapter 11: Price of 1 Bitcoin — 75

Chapter 12: Wallets vs Banks — 80

Chapter 13: Apolitical Manifesto — 85

Chapter 14: Financial Freedom — 91

Chapter 15: Inheritance Planning — 98

Chapter 16: Global Adoption vs Global Banning — 105

Chapter 17: Energy Debate — 112

Chapter 18: Noises of Altcoins — 122

Chapter 19: DeFi and dApps on Bitcoin — 129

Chapter 20: Bitcoinization — 135

Chapter 21: Into The Bitcoin Lingo — 142

Activity: Answers — 151

Preface

I had never imagined that my journey to teach beginners about Bitcoin in just 21 days would lead to a book publication. This is my first book, and it carries a lot of emotions. After six months of hard work, I am proud to present this comprehensive beginner's guide to mastering the future of money through Bitcoin, with 21 chapters and over 200 practice quizzes.

In today's digital age, understanding the future of money has become increasingly important, and Bitcoin is a prominent player in the world of finance and technology. As a decentralized digital currency, Bitcoin offers exciting opportunities for financial empowerment and innovation.

This book is specifically designed for beginners who are eager to learn and master the concepts of Bitcoin. Each day, you will delve into a new chapter, covering the fundamentals of Bitcoin technology, learning how to safely acquire, store, and transact with Bitcoin, exploring the economic implications of this digital currency, and much more. The practice quizzes provided will allow you to reinforce your understanding and test your knowledge, ensuring that you are well-equipped to grasp the concepts covered.

One unique aspect of this book is its applicability in schools, making it an excellent addition to grade 5 to 12 teachings. As Bitcoin gains more prominence in the world of finance and technology, it is essential for students to be exposed to this cutting-edge topic that can potentially shape the future of money.

With its user-friendly language, clear explanations, and practical examples, this book aims to make learning about Bitcoin accessible and enjoyable for beginners of all ages. Whether you are a student, a teacher, a parent, or simply curious about the future of money, "Bitcoin 101: Mastering the Future of Money in Just 21 Days" is your comprehensive guide to unlocking the potential of Bitcoin. So, let's embark on this exciting journey together and master the future of money with Bitcoin!

I began this project with a vision to provide easy-to-read, engaging, and visually appealing content on Bitcoin. Despite our best efforts, there may be areas that need improvement. We appreciate all comments and feedback about this book. We hope this first edition serves you well.

Krishna Dahal

Chapter 1 — Magic of Money

What is Money?

Money is a language to exchange value.

- What is money to you?
- Can we imagine a world without money?

Easy Money vs Hard Money

Easy Money	Hard Money
• Minimum effort to obtain • Encourages spending but eventually can overheat an economy • Causes inflation • Currency decreases in value	• Hard to obtain • Encourages saving • Financial Stability • Currency increases in value or remains stable
USD, NPR, Clothes, Foods, Cars	**Gold, Silver, Rai Stones, Bitcoin**

9 Qualities of Money

Money is an Abstract Concept

How something becomes money?

To become a money, it needs 4 steps of evolution.

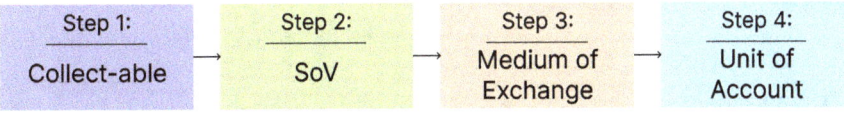

- When was the last time we shopped with commodity?

Magic of Money

Trivia To Explore

- Try to write one sentence for each of the terms.

Purchasing Power :

....

Gresham's Law :

....

Inflation :

....

Deflation :

....

Stagflation :

....

Seigniorage :

....

Demurrage :

....

Cantillon Effect :

....

Schools of Economic Philosophy

Austrian ⟶ Individual, free market (Bitcoin resonates).

Marxian ⟶ Class struggle.

Socialist ⟶ Advocating for collective or governmental ownership and administration.

Keynesian ⟶ Focuses on the role of government in managing the economy.

Public Choice ⟶ Seeks to apply economic analysis to political decision-making processes and institutions.

Neo classical ⟶ Individuals are rational and make decisions based on their own self-interest.

Which school of economic philosophy do you belong to? Think & Analyze.

Where does the value of money come from?

History of Money

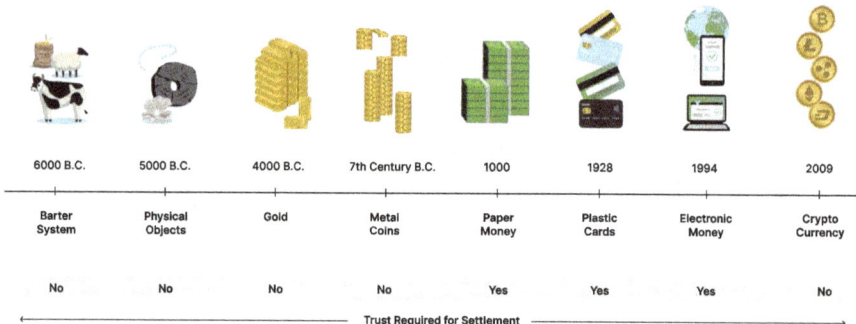

The origin of money dates back to 6000 BC, and since then, the monetary system has undergone 8 significant changes, as depicted in the figure above. Broadly we can divide the monetary system into 2 categories based on "Trust Required For Settlement":

    a. Trust Required:
        Paper money, Plastic cards, Electronic money
    b. No Trust Required:
        Barter, Commodities, Gold, Metal coins, Cryptocurrency

If the monetary system requires "trust" for settlement, the trustee controls the monetary system.

If "trust" is required, value of money comes from promises of issuer.
If "trust" is not required, value of money comes from money itself.

History of Money in Nepal

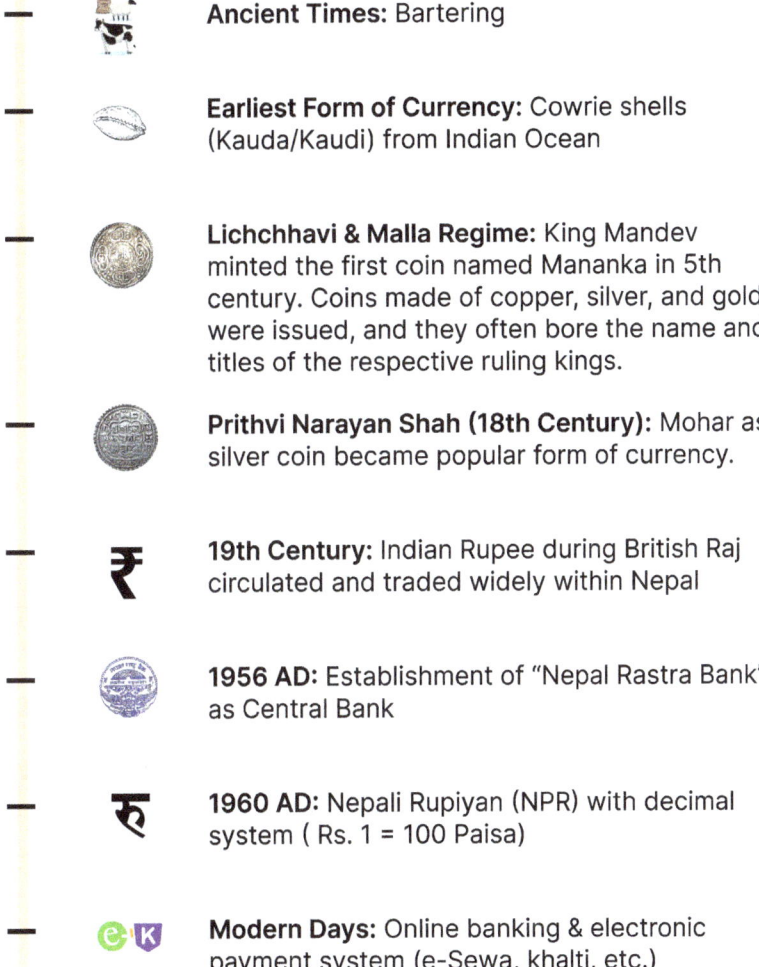

Ancient Times: Bartering

Earliest Form of Currency: Cowrie shells (Kauda/Kaudi) from Indian Ocean

Lichchhavi & Malla Regime: King Mandev minted the first coin named Mananka in 5th century. Coins made of copper, silver, and gold were issued, and they often bore the name and titles of the respective ruling kings.

Prithvi Narayan Shah (18th Century): Mohar as silver coin became popular form of currency.

19th Century: Indian Rupee during British Raj circulated and traded widely within Nepal

1956 AD: Establishment of "Nepal Rastra Bank" as Central Bank

1960 AD: Nepali Rupiyan (NPR) with decimal system (Rs. 1 = 100 Paisa)

Modern Days: Online banking & electronic payment system (e-Sewa, khalti, etc.)

In Nepalese societies, economic transactions predominantly rely on cash; debit card or credit card payments are still not common; and larger financial decisions such as buying houses, lands, educational expenses, etc., are still typically conducted without the involvement of formal banking systems or bank loans.

However, the Nepali Rupiyan (NPR), managed by the Nepal Government and Nepal Rastra Bank, has suffered of political instability and corruption, resulting in an inflated economy and exacerbating the wealth disparity between the affluent and less privileged social classes.

How We Ended Up With Debt Based Financial Model?

Before the existence of paper-based money, people utilized commodities, metals, gold, and labor as forms of currency. Intrinsic value was determined without the need for any authorities.

For efficient market, trades and wars, paper-based money was introduced. These were bills or promissory notes. Initially, issuers were kings, followed by governments and central banks.

Central banks now have the power to create money out of thin air, that created our debt-based economy. Since 1971, paper money has not been backed by any tangible assets; its value relies solely on the trust of the government. However, this trust has a history full of betrayals.

In the modern internet age, it became necessary to have something akin to digital gold as sound money. A fully functional trustless monetary system was in need. Then Bitcoin emerged in 2009 to fulfill this requirement.

What's in Bitcoin?

- Cryptography
- Digital assets (electronic)
- Borderless
- Permissionless
- Peer-to-peer
- Has no intrinsic value (debatable)
- No physical form
- No central authority

Double Spending Solved	Unit of Account
Decentralized Consensus	Proof of Ownership
Deterministic Economics	

Activity

Choose the correct answer below.

1. "Hard Money" is also known as:
   ☐ Good Money ☐ Sound Money ☐ Strong Money ☐ Easy Money

2. Which of the following is NOT a quality of money?
   ☐ Portability ☐ Divisibility ☐ Uniformity ☐ Malleability

3. Which of the following is the biggest discovery of banking system?
   ☐ Paper Money ☐ Gold backed currency ☐ Fractional Reserve ☐ Ledger System

4. Barter System failed as an inefficient system to match market order.
   ☐ True ☐ False

5. Digital Money (Khalti, PayPal, e-Sewa) settles faster than Bitcoin.
   ☐ True ☐ False

6. What is SoV?
   ☐ Secured Operating Value ☐ Sense of Value ☐ Store of Value ☐ Sender of Value

7. Bitcoin is closer to which school of economic thought?
   ☐ Marxian ☐ Austrian ☐ Keynesian ☐ Classical

Activity

8. Which of the following term defines different propagation rate of price changes on assets when money supply changes?

   ☐ Cantillon Effect ☐ Gresham's Law ☐ Demurrage ☐ Stagflation

9. Cryptocurrency has intrinsic value. True or False?

   ☐ True ☐ False ☐ Debatable

10. Inflation rate of bitcoin in 2100 A.D. is:

    ☐ Can't be defined ☐ Bitcoin has no inflation ☐ 3.56% ☐ 0.000002984%

Chapter 2: Finding Satoshi Nakamoto

Who is Satoshi Nakamoto?

- **Creator of Bitcoin**
- Active Years on Bitcoin:
  10/31/2008 – 12/13/2010 (772 days)
- Writing: British English
- Sleeping hours: Matches England's time
- P2P Foundation Profile: 47 years old, Male, Japan

- **Genesis Block Message**
  The Times 03/Jan/2009 Chancellor on brink of second bailout for banks

Flash Back on e-Cash

Bitcoin is an outcome of 30 years of research.

- **1983**: David Chaum's e-Cash/DigiCash
- **1997** : Adam Back's "Hash Cash".
- **1998** : Wei Dai's "B-Money".
- **1998** : Nick Szabo's "Bit Gold" &
- **2004** : Hal Finney's "Reusable Proof of Work".

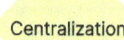

> **Link to Explore**
> https://en.wikipedia.org/wiki/Cypherpunk

First Appearance of Satoshi

> "I've been working on a new electronic cash system that's fully peer-to-peer, with no trusted third party."

- Bitcoin Whitepaper Released : October 31, 2008

- Cryptography mailing list

  Link to Explore
  https://satoshi.nakamotoinstitute.org/emails/

- Was that young Satoshi in 1999?
  https://marc.info/?l=cypherpunks&m=95280154629912&w=2

Personality of Satoshi

- Philosophical
- Excellent knowledge of computer science, cryptography, economics, monetary system, game theory, and government.
- Well versed in English.
- Serious about work. No joking around.
- Average programming skill

Finding Satoshi Nakamoto

Top Satoshi Quotes

> If you don't believe it or don't get it, I don't have the time to try to convince you, sorry.

> The root problem with conventional currency is all the trust that's required to make it work. The central bank must be trusted not to debase the currency, but the history of fiat currencies is full of breaches of that trust.

> It might make sense just to get some in case it catches on. If enough people think the same way, that becomes a self-fulfilling prophecy.

> The nature of Bitcoin is such that once version 0.1 was released, the core design was set in stone for the rest of its lifetime.

Link to Explore
https://satoshi.nakamotoinstitute.org/posts/

> Lost coins only make everyone else's coins worth slightly more. Think of it as a donation to everyone.

> Governments are good at cutting off the heads of a centrally controlled networks like Napster, but pure P2P networks like Gnutella and Tor seem to be holding their own.

> It would have been nice to get this attention in any other context. WikiLeaks has kicked the hornet's nest, and the swarm is headed towards us.

Identity of Satoshi

No one knows who Satoshi was.

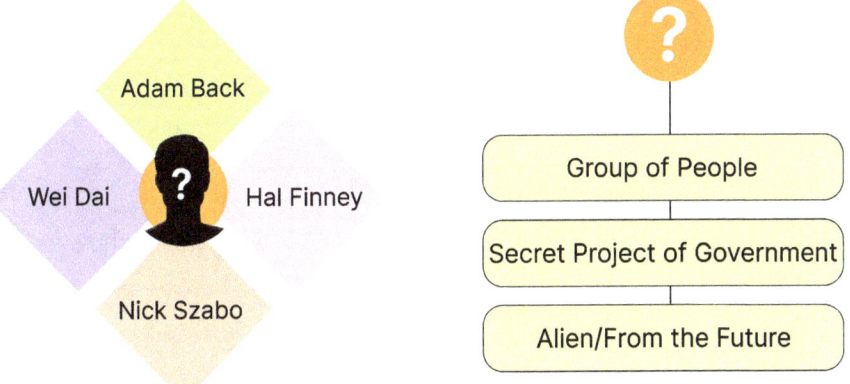

Disappearance of Satoshi

> **12/13/2010**
> It would have been nice to get this attention in any other context. WikiLeaks has kicked the hornet's nest, and the swarm is headed towards us.

Maintainers of Bitcoin Core

Satoshi Nakamoto	Gavin Andresen	Wladimir van der Laan
1/3/09 - 2/23/11	2/23/11 - 4/7/14	4/7/14 - Present

We are all, Satoshi!

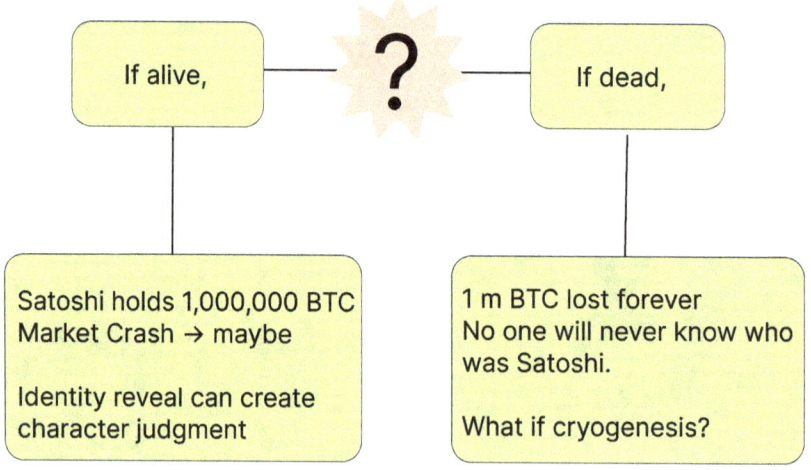

If alive,
Satoshi holds 1,000,000 BTC
Market Crash → maybe

Identity reveal can create character judgment

If dead,
1 m BTC lost forever
No one will never know who was Satoshi.

What if cryogenesis?

Finding Satoshi Nakamoto

Activity

Choose the correct answer below.

1. What was the pseudonym used by the creator of Bitcoin?

   ☐ John Doe ☐ Satoshi Nakamoto ☐ James Smith ☐ Michael Johnson

2. How many bitcoins did Satoshi Nakamoto own when he disappeared?

   ☐ 0 ☐ 10,000 ☐ 100,000 ☐ 1 million

3. What was the last known communication from Satoshi Nakamoto?

   ☐ An email to a Bitcoin developer
   ☐ A post on the Bitcoin forum
   ☐ A tweet
   ☐ A video interview

4. Who was the first person to receive a Bitcoin transaction from Satoshi Nakamoto?

   ☐ Hal Finney ☐ Nick Szabo ☐ Craig Wright ☐ Dorian Nakamoto

5. What was the first item ever purchased with Bitcoin?

   ☐ Pizza ☐ Computer ☐ Car ☐ Plane ticket

6. Who is considered as Father of Cryptocurrency?

   ☐ Steve Jobs ☐ David Chaum ☐ Adam Back ☐ Nick Szabo

7. What is the name of the person who claimed to be Satoshi Nakamoto in 2014?

   ☐ Craig Wright ☐ Hal Finney ☐ Nick Szabo ☐ Dorian Nakamoto

Activity

8. What was the original purpose of Bitcoin according to Satoshi Nakamoto?

   ☐ To create a decentralized digital currency
   ☐ To disrupt the banking industry
   ☐ To provide a new way to make online payments
   ☐ To replace traditional currencies

9. What was the first version of the Bitcoin software called?

   ☐ Bitcoin Core   ☐ Bitcoin Classic   ☐ Bitcoin XT   ☐ Bitcoin Legacy

10. Based on daily inactive pattern of Satoshi Nakamoto, select the closest nationality he might belong to?

    ☐ India   ☐ Japan   ☐ UK   ☐ USA

11. What does "bitcoin" and "Bitcoin" represent?

    ☐ Both are same
    ☐ "bitcoin" is network; "Bitcoin" is cryptocurrency
    ☐ "Bitcoin" is network; "bitcoin" is cryptocurrency
    ☐ Satoshi renamed legacy version to "Bitcoin" from "bitcoin" after launch.

Chapter 3 — Capping the World at 21 Million

All is Wealth!

- Total Wealth = 464 trillion USD
- 62.5 m millionaires
- 1.2% controls 47.8% of wealth
- 53.2% controls 1.1% of wealth

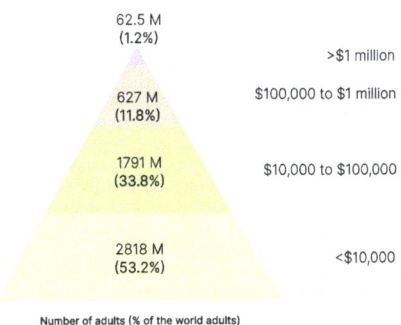

One person's income is another person's expense.

What Do You Own?

- Money in the form of cash makes 3% of wealth.
- Gold makes 2.6% of wealth
- Bitcoin makes 0.21% of wealth

Inflationary vs Deflationary World

Inflationary World	Deflationary World
• Increase in prices of goods and services	• Decrease in prices of goods and services
• Encourage spending	• Encourage hoarding
• (a) goods & services supply is decreasing, or (b) there is more money in the market to make the purchase	• (a) goods & services supply is increasing, or (b) there is less money in the market to make the purchase
• Hyperinflation	• Deflationary death spiral
• Extreme example: 2007-2009 Financial Crisis	• Extreme example: Japan 1991-2001

Learn about: CPI (consumer price index)
Bitcoin works in disinflation model

- Governments and central banks often employ inflationary models to stimulate economic growth and avoid deflationary spirals.

- It's important to note that both inflation and deflation can have significant impacts on an economy, and finding the right balance is often a challenge

21,000,000 BTC Hard Cap

Average block time of 10 minutes

Reward: $50 + 25 + 12.5 + 6.25 + .. = \sum_{n=1}^{\infty} 25 \times 2^{2-n} = 100$

Cycle: $6 * 24 * 365 * 4 = 210{,}240 \sim 210{,}000$

Hard Cap = $100 * 210{,}000 = 21{,}000{,}000$

Reward Cycle starts with 50 BTC

Bitcoin's heart beats at every 10 minutes. New block is produced, and new bitcoins are rewarded to miner until all 21,000,000 BTC are mined.

In 2009, bitcoin block started with 50 BTC reward. In 2025, bitcoin block reward is 3.125 BTC.

Bitcoin has a fixed maximum supply of 21 million coins, which cannot be altered without agreement from the network's participants.

Link to Explore

- https://github.com/bitcoin/bitcoin/blob/f436bfd126adaa64daba2e78016eb707e37eabce/src/chainparams.cpp
- https://github.com/bitcoin/bitcoin/blob/master/src/validation.cpp#L1501

Capping the World at 21 Million

Mathematically Deterministic

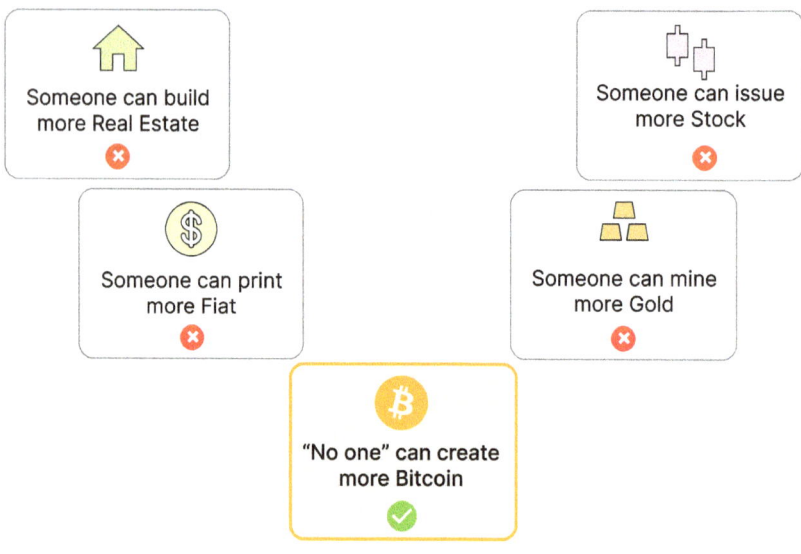

In Case It Catches On

> It might make sense just to get some in case it catches on. If enough people think the same way, that becomes a self-fulfilling prophecy.

Link to Explore

- https://satoshi.nakamotoinstitute.org/emails/bitcoin-list/threads/4/
- https://satoshi.nakamotoinstitute.org/emails/cryptography/17/#selection-103.0-107.9

Capping the World at 21 Million

At The End of Mining 21,000,000th BTC

This shows Bitcoin Block 775043 and its content. Miner gets Subsidy + fees. At the end of block reward, network transaction fees will motivate miners.

Source: Mempool.Space

```
It's interesting that the system can be configured to only allow a
certain maximum number of coins ever to be generated. I guess the idea
is that the amount of work needed to generate a new coin will become
more difficult as time goes on.

One immediate problem with any new currency is how to value it. Even
ignoring the practical problem that virtually no one will accept it at
first, there is still a difficulty in coming up with a reasonable
argument in favor of a particular non-zero value for the coins.

As an amusing thought experiment, imagine that Bitcoin is successful
and becomes the dominant payment system in use throughout the world.
Then the total value of the currency should be equal to the total
value of all the wealth in the world. Current estimates of total
worldwide household wealth that I have found range from $100 trillion
to $300 trillion. With 20 million coins, that gives each coin a value
of about $10 million.

So the possibility of generating coins today with a few cents of
compute time may be quite a good bet, with a payoff of something like
100 million to 1! Even if the odds of Bitcoin succeeding to this
degree are slim, are they really 100 million to one against? Something
to think about...

Hal
```

Capping the World at 21 Million

Activity

Choose the correct answer below.

1. What is the maximum number of bitcoins that will ever exist?
   - [ ] 10 million
   - [ ] 21 million
   - [ ] 50 million
   - [ ] Unlimited

2. Why is the 21 million bitcoin limit important?
   - [ ] It ensures a stable value for bitcoin
   - [ ] It prevents inflation
   - [ ] It maintains scarcity
   - [ ] All of the above

3. When is it estimated that all 21 million bitcoins will be mined?
   - [ ] 2140
   - [ ] 2060
   - [ ] 2080
   - [ ] 2100

4. What happens when all 21 million bitcoins have been mined?
   - [ ] No new bitcoins can be created
   - [ ] The value of bitcoin will decrease
   - [ ] Bitcoin mining will become easier
   - [ ] All of the above

5. Who created the 21 million bitcoin limit?
   - [ ] Satoshi Nakamoto
   - [ ] Vitalik Buterin
   - [ ] Gavin Andresen
   - [ ] Charlie Lee

6. How many bitcoins have been mined as of 2023?
   - [ ] 16 million
   - [ ] 19 million
   - [ ] 20 million
   - [ ] 21 million

Activity

7. How does the 21 million bitcoin limit compare to traditional fiat currencies?
   - [ ] Fiat currencies have a fixed limit like bitcoin
   - [ ] Fiat currencies have an unlimited supply
   - [ ] Fiat currencies have a limit, but it can be changed by central banks
   - [ ] Fiat currencies have a limit, but it is not publicly known

8. How does the 21 million bitcoin limit affect transaction fees?
   - [ ] Transaction fees will decrease as bitcoin becomes more scarce
   - [ ] Transaction fees will increase as bitcoin becomes more scarce
   - [ ] Transaction fees will remain the same regardless of bitcoin supply
   - [ ] Transaction fees will be eliminated once all bitcoins have been mined

9. What is the significance of the 21 million number?
   - [ ] It is a random number chosen by Satoshi Nakamoto
   - [ ] It represents the maximum number of people who can use bitcoin
   - [ ] It is based on the maximum number of bits that can be represented by a computer
   - [ ] It is a deliberate choice to ensure scarcity and maintain value

10. Can the 21 million bitcoin limit be changed?
    - [ ] Yes, it can be changed by bitcoin nodes with consensus
    - [ ] No, it is a hard-coded limit that cannot be changed
    - [ ] Yes, it can be changed by a single person with enough computing power
    - [ ] Yes, it can be changed by bitcoin miners.

Chapter 4 — Halving Supply Shock

What is Bitcoin Halving?

An event when the reward for mining bitcoin transactions is cut in half.

Rules of Bitcoin Halving

- Creation of new bitcoin reduces by 50% at every 210,000 blocks.
- Creation of new bitcoin starts with 50 BTC per block.
- There will be maximum of 33 halving events.
- 210,000 blocks ~ 210,000 / (6 * 24 * 365) ~ 4 years.
- 50 BTC ~ 25 BTC ~ 12.5 BTC ~ 6.25 BTC ~ 3.125 BTC ....
- $\sum_{n=1}^{\infty} 25 \times 2^{2-n} = 100$

Effects of Bitcoin Halving

- Game of Supply & Demand
- New BTC availability goes down with time
- Time tested asset gets increased adoption
- Increase in adoption means more demand
- Growth of miners & network effects
- Cost to produce new BTC increases independently
- Price Impact (Price Appreciation)

Inflation Rate of Bitcoin

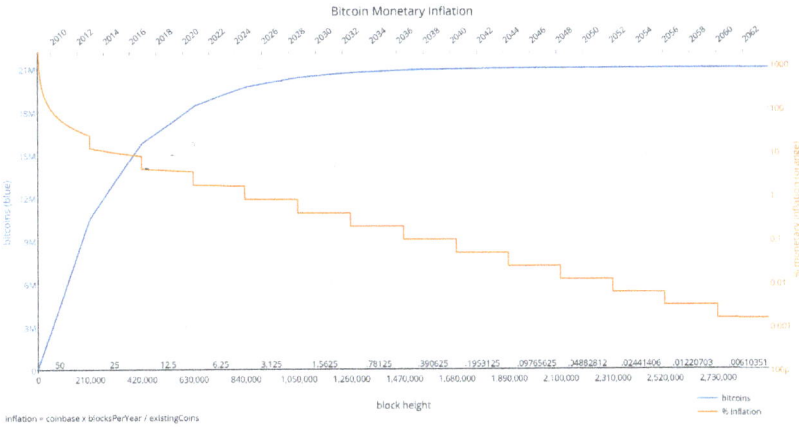

Image Source : Cointelegraph (World's Best Performing Currency : Bitcoin Inflation Rate Drops to 4%

Bitcoin's economy is mathematically deterministic and verifiable by anyone. Inflation rate goes down every four year and stops on year 2140 AD.

What is the current inflation rate of Bitcoin? **Calculate.**

Halving Supply Shock

Halving to Flow Model (H2F)

Halving Events	Dates	Halving Price → Next	Mining Hashrate
1st Halving (25)	Nov 28, 2012	$12 (x25) → 300	27.15 * 10^12
2nd Halving (12.5)	July 9, 2016	$647 (x12.5) → 8087	1.60 * 10^18 H/s
3rd Halving (6.25)	May 11, 2020	$8566 (x6.25) → 53,537	115.86 * 10^18 H/s
4th Halving (3.125)	April, 2024	$63500 (x3.125) → $198,437.5	633.99 * 10^18 H/s
5th Halving	TBD, 2028	?? (x1.5625) →	??
6th Halving	TBD, 2032	??	??

Based on past 3 halving events, disinflation model of bitcoin seems to create supply shock in the market. Increasing mining hash rate shows growth on network effect as price appreciation goes multi-folds.
Halving Price → Next is experimented to guess next halving price. As shown in table, price of BTC during 2024 halving was predicted around $53k (actual $63.5k). For 2028 halving price is expected to be $198.4k.

> Guess the price of BTC at next halving event?
> Read more on H2F Model: https://bit.ly/3PuyeeR

Every four year, bitcoin halving event occurs and disinflation happens. Within few months of this event, price history shows aggressive uptrend. 5th halving will happen in 2028.

Halving Supply Shock

Final Halving Event

- Final Halving Event will occur on 2140 (117 years to go)
- Guaranteed by code.

```
Bitcoin halving (line 1093)
<> bitcoin-halving.cpp
 1    CAmount GetBlockSubsidy(int nHeight, const Consensus::Params& consensusParams)
 2    {
 3        int halvings = nHeight / consensusParams.nSubsidyHalvingInterval;
 4        // Force block reward to zero when right shift is undefined.
 5        if (halvings >= 64)
 6            return 0;
 7
 8        CAmount nSubsidy = 50 * COIN;
 9        // Subsidy is cut in half every 210,000 blocks which will occur approximately every 4 years.
10        nSubsidy >>= halvings;
11        return nSubsidy;
12    }
```

Often misinterpreted as "there will be 64 Bitcoin halvings". Why?

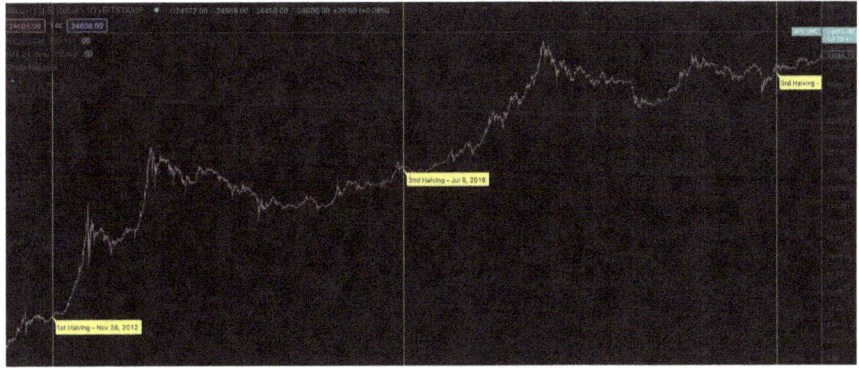

Halving Supply Shock

Activity

Choose the correct answer below.

1. What is "halving event" in Bitcoin?

   ☐ A process by which new bitcoins are created
   ☐ A process by which transaction fees are reduced
   ☐ A process by which the mining reward is reduced by half
   ☐ None of the above

2. What is the purpose of the halving event in Bitcoin?

   ☐ To increase the supply of bitcoins
   ☐ To reduce the number of miners on the network
   ☐ To control the inflation of bitcoin
   ☐ None of the above

3. When was the first halving event in Bitcoin?

   ☐ 2009 ☐ 2012 ☐ 2016 ☐ None of the above

4. What is the total number of bitcoins that will ever be mined?

   ☐ 10 million ☐ 21 million ☐ 100 million ☐ None of the above

5. What is the expected impact of the halving event on the price of Bitcoin?

   ☐ The price will increase
   ☐ The price will decrease
   ☐ The price will remain the same
   ☐ None of the above

Halving Supply Shock

Activity

6. Why does the halving event have an impact on the price of Bitcoin?
   - [ ] It reduces the supply of new bitcoins
   - [ ] It increases the demand for bitcoins
   - [ ] Both a) and b)
   - [ ] None of the above

7. How did the price of Bitcoin respond to the 2012 halving event?
   - [ ] It increased significantly
   - [ ] It decreased significantly
   - [ ] It remained the same
   - [ ] None of the above

8. How many halving events can be there in Bitcoin?
   - [ ] 4
   - [ ] 33
   - [ ] Can't be defined
   - [ ] 64

9. What is the next estimated date for the halving event in Bitcoin?
   - [ ] 2021
   - [ ] 2022
   - [ ] 2023
   - [ ] 2024

10. How often does the halving event occur in Bitcoin?
    - [ ] Every 2 years
    - [ ] Every 4 years
    - [ ] Every 6 years
    - [ ] None of the above

Chapter 5 — Proof of Work vs Out of Thin Air

Out of Thin Air

- Cost of Government Issued Currency

  📄 Paper   🖨 Ink   👤 Worker

- To print $100, it costs 17.0 cents per note.
- Cost to attack: negligible, unpredictable
- Modes of attack: Server hack, physical damage, policy change

Proof of Work

- Bitcoin runs on proof-of-work (PoW) consensus mechanism to validate transactions and secure the network.

Electricity Cost in Nepal	$0.11/kWh
Electricity to mine 1 BTC	427,272 kW
1 BTC Mining Power Cost	$47000

Cost to attack: $4.5m /hr

https://www.crypto51.app/

As per 2025

Link to Explore

https://whattomine.com/coins/1-btc-sha-256?hr=140.0&p=3010.0&fee=0.5&cost=0.05&cost_currency=USD&hcost=10000&span_br=1h&span_d=&commit=Calculate

Block of Bitcoin

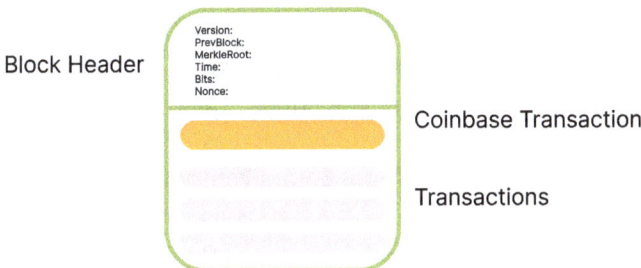

Every block has 2 components:

   a. Block Header   b. Transaction List

Transaction List has 2 types of transactions:

- Coinbase transaction: freshly minted BTC reward record to block miner.
- Transactions: sent/received BTC records (can be empty)

Block Header has 6 informations:

- **Version**: version of the bitcoin core software
- **PrevBlock**: hash of previous block
- **Merkleroot**: hash of each transaction of this block
- **Time**: timestamp of block mined
- **Bits**: a target value to mine this block
- **Nonce**: random value to change to mine.

How Block Gets Mined?

- Node receives bitcoin transactions in Mempool
- Node starts making Candidate Block from mempool transactions
- All info of that block (block header + transactions) is hashed through SHA-256 algorithm 2 times = Blockhash
- If blockhash <= target (from Bits), block is mined and added to chain.
- If not, miner needs to change the nonce and generate new blockhash

Bitcoin Core

- Bitcoin software
- https://bitcoin.org/en/bitcoin-core/
- Bitcoin developers propose new changes; fix bugs and release updates.

Mining & Mining Pools

Solo mining: Dedicating proof-of-work to mine bitcoin and getting all reward oneself.

Pool mining: Mining in a group and dividing reward based on contribution in the group.

Difficulty Adjustment Game Theory

- Every 2016 blocks, the target value changes based on participants.
- Maintains 10 minutes of average blocktime.

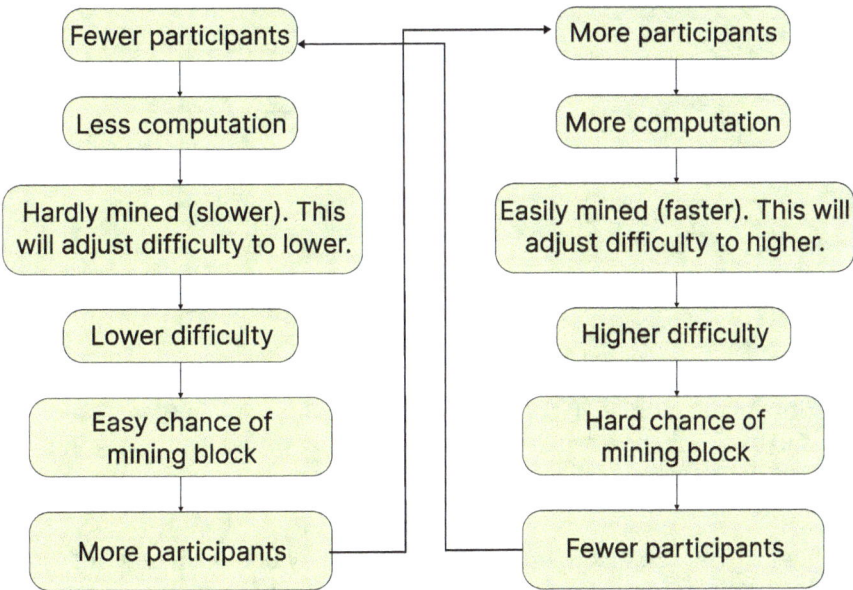

Demo of Blockchain

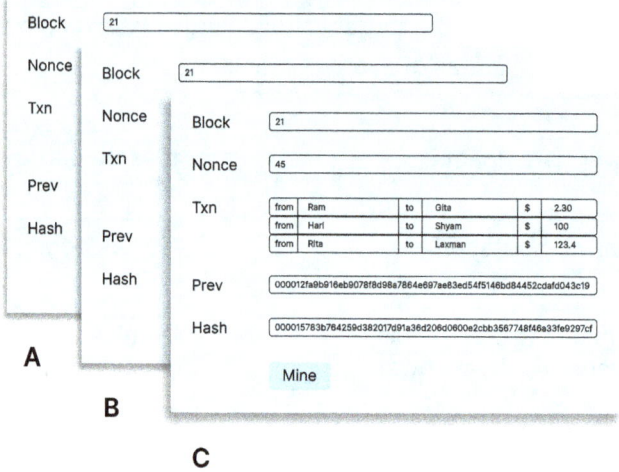

Changing anything in the past, changes everything in Blockchain and every change requires another proof-of-work. And everyone needs to agree (50% majority) for the change.

Peer A, B, C are unknown to each other. They communicate but don't rely on trust. They always try to sync up with each other and keep all the mined record of blocks.

That's why it's called Blockchain (immutable records with timestamp).

Importance of Proof-of-Work

- Energy locked digital assets (bitcoin) through immutability
- Security of bitcoin network
- Decentralization
- Double-spending prevention
- Predictable and steady rate of new bitcoin creation
- Incentivization

Link to Explore
- https://bitcoin.org/en/bitcoin-core/
-
- https://andersbrownworth.com/blockchain/hash

Activity

Choose the correct answer below.

1. What is the primary purpose of the proof of work algorithm in Bitcoin?

   ☐ To generate new bitcoins
   ☐ To validate transactions
   ☐ To secure the network against attacks
   ☐ None of the above

2. What is the name of the process by which miners compete to solve a cryptographic puzzle and add a block to the Bitcoin blockchain?

   ☐ Hashing ☐ Mining ☐ Proof of stake ☐ PoAP

3. Which of the following is a drawback of the proof of work algorithm?

   ☐ It requires a lot of computational power
   ☐ It can be easily manipulated
   ☐ It is not secure
   ☐ None of the above

4. Which of the following is a reward for miners who successfully solve the cryptographic puzzle and add a block to the blockchain?

   ☐ A fixed amount of bitcoins
   ☐ A percentage of the transaction fees
   ☐ BTC Miami Annual Ticket
   ☐ Both (a) and (b)

Activity

5. Which of the following factors affects the difficulty of the proof of work algorithm?
   - [ ] The number of miners on the network
   - [ ] Leap year calendar
   - [ ] Block size
   - [ ] Speed of mining hardware

6. What is the name of the protocol upgrade that reduced the mining reward from 50 BTC to 25 BTC in 2012?
   - [ ] Segregated Witness (SegWit)
   - [ ] Lightning Network
   - [ ] Halving
   - [ ] Taproot

7. What is the term used to describe the method by which new Fiat currency is created?
   - [ ] Proof of work
   - [ ] Out of thin air
   - [ ] Proof of stake
   - [ ] None of the above

9. What is the name of the process by which transactions are bundled together and added to the blockchain as a new block?
   - [ ] Segregation
   - [ ] Aggregation
   - [ ] Hashing
   - [ ] None of the above

8. Which of the following is a potential security threat to the proof of work algorithm?
   - [ ] A 51% attack
   - [ ] A Sybil attack
   - [ ] Both a) and b)
   - [ ] None of the above

10. What is the name of the process by which the proof of work algorithm is adjusted to ensure a consistent rate of block creation?
    - [ ] Mining adjustment
    - [ ] Hashing adjustment
    - [ ] Difficulty adjustment
    - [ ] Block reorganization

Chapter 6 | Becoming a Node. Verify, Don't Trust

What is Bitcoin Node?

- Computers running Bitcoin Core
- Communicating with each other

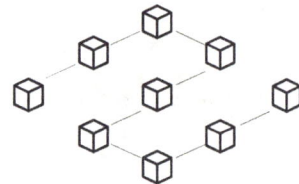

What does Bitcoin Node do?

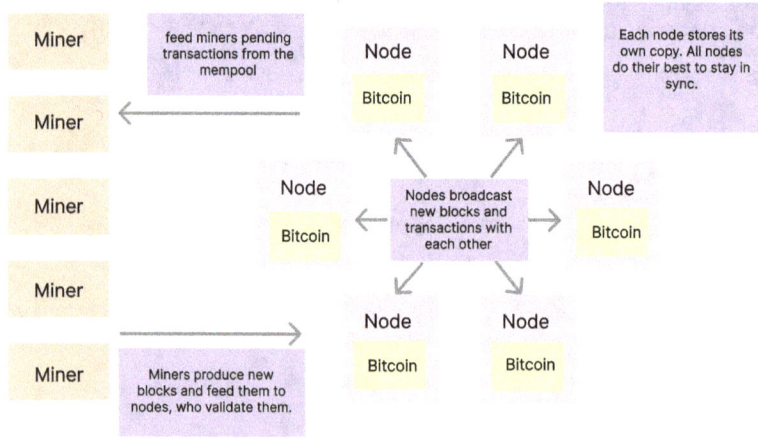

Types of Bitcoin Node

- Full node: stores all blocks info
- Lightweight node: keeps only block header info to query
- Mining node: mines and confirms the new block

> **Link to Explore**
> - https://bitcoin.design/guide/how-it-works/nodes/

Why to run a Bitcoin Node

1. **Verify Bitcoin's supply:** By running a Bitcoin node, individuals can autonomously verify the current state of the Bitcoin network, ensuring the accuracy and transparency of its supply.

2. **Prevent double spending:** A node acts as a safeguard against fraudulent activities like double spending, automatically rejecting any bitcoins that have already been spent before, ensuring the integrity of transactions.

3. **Independence from third parties:** Running a node empowers users to transact in Bitcoin directly, without relying on intermediaries. Users can broadcast and verify their own transactions, enhancing privacy, security, and control over their financial activities.

4. **Strengthen the Bitcoin network:** Another incentive for running a full node is to contribute to the overall resilience and robustness of the Bitcoin network, reinforcing its stability and decentralization.

Which Node, Which Feature?

	Confirms New Blocks	Verifies New Transactions	Has a Wallet	Keeps a full copy of Bitcoin
Light Nodes	✗	✓	✓	✗
Full Nodes	✗	✓	✓	✓
Mining Nodes	✓	✗	✗	✗

How to run a Bitcoin Node?

- Prerequisite: Internet/No-internet, computer, 600 GB storage
- GUI Software: Download from https://bitcoin.org/en/download
- Command line: https://github.com/bitcoin/bitcoin/blob/master/doc/build-osx.md
- Node-in-a-Box: https://blockstream.com/satellite/ https://umbrel.com/ https://github.com/bavarianledger/bitcoin-nodes

Becoming a Node. Verify, Don't Trust

Step-by-step guide on how to run a Bitcoin node (7 Steps):

1. Set up the necessary hardware:
   - Choose a computer with sufficient processing power & storage.
   - Ensure a stable internet connection with sufficient bandwidth.

2. Install the Bitcoin Core software:
   - Visit the official Bitcoin Core website (bitcoincore.org) and download the software compatible with your operating system.
   - Follow the installation instructions provided for your specific operating system.

3. Download the Bitcoin blockchain:
   - Launch the Bitcoin Core software.
   - Allow the software to synchronize with the Bitcoin network by downloading the entire blockchain. This process may take a significant amount of time, as the blockchain is quite large.

4. Configure the Bitcoin node:
   - Access the Bitcoin Core software's settings to customize your node's behavior and preferences.
   - Set up the data directory where the blockchain and other data will be stored.

5. Enable port forwarding (optional):
   - If you want your Bitcoin node to accept incoming connections from other nodes, configure your router to enable port forwarding for the Bitcoin network port (default is 8333).

6. Start running the Bitcoin node:
    - Launch the Bitcoin Core software, and it will begin running as a Bitcoin node.
    - Allow the software to continuously synchronize with the network to stay up to date with the latest transactions and blocks.

7. Maintain and update your Bitcoin node:
    - Regularly update your Bitcoin Core software to the latest version to ensure you have the latest security patches and improvements.
    - Keep your hardware and internet connection running reliably to maintain the node's availability.

Do I earn from running a Bitcoin Node?

- Simple answer: No
- Yes, if you start mining.

Link to Explore
- https://bitnodes.io/nodes/live-map/

Activity

Choose the correct answer below.

1. What is a Bitcoin node?

- [ ] A type of cryptocurrency wallet
- [ ] A computer that runs the Bitcoin software and participates in the network
- [ ] A type of Bitcoin transaction
- [ ] None of the above

2. Why is it important to run your own Bitcoin node?

- [ ] To support the decentralization of the Bitcoin network
- [ ] To verify your own transactions and avoid reliance on third-party services
- [ ] To improve network security and privacy
- [ ] All of the above

3. What are the hardware requirements for running a Bitcoin node?

- [ ] A high-end computer with a fast internet connection with 400 GB storage
- [ ] A dedicated server with a 1 TB of storage space but no internet
- [ ] A Raspberry Pi or other low-cost computer with 1 TB storage and internet
- [ ] None of the above

4. What is the role of a Bitcoin node in the network?

- [ ] To process transactions and create new bitcoins
- [ ] To validate and relay transactions and blocks to other nodes
- [ ] To perform complex calculations to solve cryptographic puzzles
- [ ] None of the above

> **Activity**

5. How can you verify the integrity of the Bitcoin software running on your node?

   ☐ By downloading the software from a trusted source and comparing its hash with the official release
   ☐ By trusting the Bitcoin community to verify the software for you
   ☐ By running the software and assuming it is legitimate
   ☐ None of the above

6. How can you check that your Bitcoin node is properly connected to the network?

   ☐ By checking the number of connected nodes on your node's dashboard
   ☐ By sending a small test transaction and verifying that it is confirmed on the network
   ☐ By running a network diagnostic tool like Ping or TraceRoute
   ☐ None of the above

7. What is the difference between a full node and a light node?

   ☐ A full node stores the entire Bitcoin blockchain, while a light node only stores a portion of it
   ☐ A full node is more secure and private than a light node
   ☐ A full node requires more computing power and storage space than a light node
   ☐ All of the above

8. What are the benefits of running a full node instead of a light node?

   ☐ Increased security and privacy
   ☐ Greater control over your Bitcoin transactions and data
   ☐ Ability to participate in Bitcoin's consensus process and vote on changes to the protocol
   ☐ All of the above

Activity

9. What is the risk of trusting a third-party service to validate your Bitcoin transactions?

   ☐ The service may not properly validate your transactions, leading to lost funds
   ☐ The service may be hacked or compromised, leading to theft of your Bitcoin
   ☐ The service may impose fees or restrictions on your Bitcoin transactions
   ☐ All of the above

10. What is the famous quote associated with running a Bitcoin node?

    ☐ "Not your keys, not your Bitcoin"
    ☐ "Don't trust, verify"
    ☐ "HODL"
    ☐ "If you don't believe me or don't get it, I don't have time to try to convince you, sorry."

Chapter 7 — Civil War of 2017

With Great Power, Comes Great Responsibility

- **Trilemma of Blockchain:**
  One feature gets always compromised among decentralization, security and scalability.

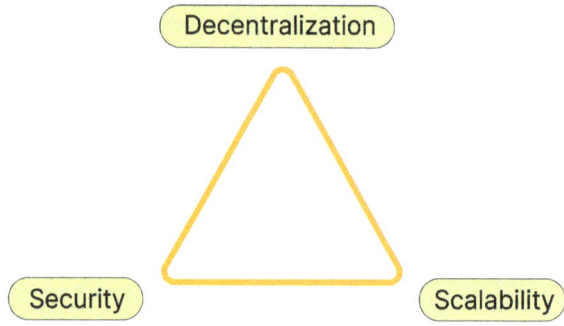

- No one controls Bitcoin – and that is a great power
- But different people have different opinions
- How bitcoin grows? Who takes the decision? Who fixes Bitcoin if broken?

Forks

Since no one controls Bitcoin blockchain, anyone can propose new changes.

If someone desires to make alterations to an existing chain, there are two possible outcomes: either a consensus is reached to upgrade the chain, or the consensus fails and a separate branch, known as a Fork, is created.

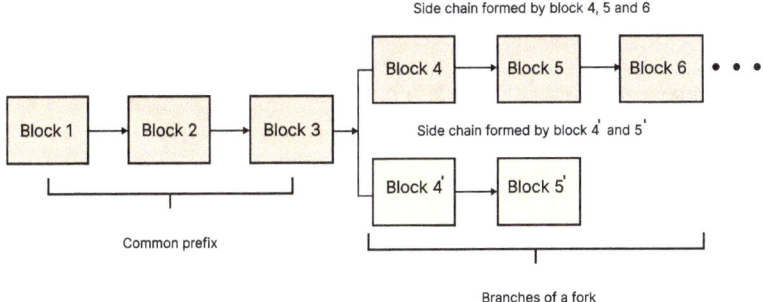

Branches of a fork

- Soft Fork: Backward compatible | Same coin
- Hard Fork: Backward in-compatible | New coin

Blocksize History

- Satoshi started with 32 mb [p2p block message max limit]
- Satoshi lowered it to 1 mb at 79,400 blocks; never told why.
- Speculation: to process the block faster, anti-spam measure against overloading network with bogus transactions, temporary measure
- As time went up, bitcoin network got more adoptions, more transactions and block size filling increased up and up
- Some supported to lift this block size limit; some went against

Big Blockers vs Small Blockers

Why we Bigger Block size	Why we need Smaller Block size
- More TPS - Not enough space now so txn fee war - For mass adoption	- Big block increases cost for nodes to store - Big block needs more bandwidth to download - Bigger block creates risk of centralized mining

Civil War of 2017

History of Fork Wars

2014: Bitcoin XT
- 1000 nodes joined but ceased after Summer 2015
- 8 MB block size for 24 TPS

2016: Bitcoin Classic
- For 2 MB block size

2016: Bitcoin Unlimited
- Up to 16 MB

2017: Bitcoin Cash
- 8 MB block size + rejection of SegWit
- Roger Van, Craig Wright → Bitcoin SV fork in 2018

2017: Bitcoin Gold
- made for GPU

Intended Hard Forks (3)

- **Bitcoin Cash:** Created to increase the block size limit and allow for more transactions per block.
- **Bitcoin Gold:** Created to make mining more accessible to average users by using GPU mining instead of ASICs.
- **Bitcoin SV:** Created to restore the original Satoshi Vision of Bitcoin and increase the block size to 128 MB.

Soft Forks (16)

- **BIP 16 (P2SH):** Allowed for more complex scripts and added support for multisig transactions.
- **BIP 30:** Changed the way duplicate transactions were handled in the blockchain.
- **BIP 34:** Introduced the concept of block height into the Bitcoin protocol.
- **BIP 37 (Bloom filters):** Improved how lightweight wallets received transaction information.
- **BIP 65:** Enabled the use of the CHECKLOCKTIMEVERIFY opcode to allow for time-locked transactions.
- **BIP 66:** Increased the security of the digital signatures used in Bitcoin transactions.
- **BIP 68:** Defined a new sequence number field to enable relative time-locks.
- **BIP 112:** Enabled the use of the OP_CHECKSEQUENCEVERIFY opcode for time-locked transactions.

- **BIP 113:** Enabled the use of the OP_CHECKLOCKTIMEVERIFY opcode for time-locked transactions.
- **BIP 141 (SegWit):** Separated transaction signatures from transaction data to increase the block size limit.
- **BIP 143:** Improved the digital signature algorithm used in Bitcoin transactions.
- **BIP 147:** Improved the security of the digital signature algorithm used in Bitcoin transactions.
- **BIP 173 (Bech32):** Introduced a new address format for greater compatibility with future upgrades.
- **BIP 340:** Introduced the Schnorr signature algorithm to improve transaction privacy and reduce fees.
- **BIP 341:** Enabled the use of Taproot, a new scripting language that enables greater privacy and scalability.
- **BIP 342:** Improved the efficiency of signature hashing in Taproot transactions.

End of War

- Bitcoin continued with network growth
- Bitcoin forks disappeared one by one
- Soft forks seem preferred by community: Segwit (2016); Taproot (2020)
- Bitcoin community is now focused on L2 like Lightning

Activity

Choose the correct answer below.

1. What was the main point of disagreement in the bitcoin block size debate?

   ☐ The maximum size of a single block in the blockchain
   ☐ The maximum number of transactions per block
   ☐ The rate of block creation
   ☐ The minimum transaction fee required to include a transaction in a block

2. Which of the following was the first major fork of Bitcoin?

   ☐ Bitcoin Cash   ☐ Bitcoin Gold   ☐ Bitcoin Diamond   ☐ Bitcoin SV

3. What was the main reason for the creation of Bitcoin Cash?

   ☐ To increase the maximum block size and allow for more transactions per block
   ☐ To decrease the maximum block size and make the network more decentralized
   ☐ To introduce a new consensus algorithm to replace proof-of-work
   ☐ To implement new privacy features to make transactions more anonymous

4. Which of the following is not a major fork of Bitcoin?

   ☐ Litecoin   ☐ Bitcoin Cash   ☐ Bitcoin Gold   ☐ Bitcoin Private

5. What was the main reason for the creation of Bitcoin Gold?

   ☐ To increase the maximum block size and allow for more transactions per block
   ☐ To decrease the maximum block size and make the network more decentralized
   ☐ To implement a new consensus algorithm to replace proof-of-work
   ☐ To make Bitcoin mining more accessible to average users by using GPU mining instead of ASICs

Activity

6. What was the main reason for the creation of Bitcoin Diamond?

    ☐ To increase the maximum block size and allow for more transactions per block
    ☐ To decrease the maximum block size and make the network more decentralized
    ☐ To implement a new consensus algorithm to replace proof-of-work
    ☐ To introduce new privacy features to make transactions more anonymous

7. What is the name of the controversial scaling proposal that split the Bitcoin community in 2017?

    ☐ SegWit   ☐ Lightning Network   ☐ Bitcoin Unlimited   ☐ Bitcoin Core

8. Which of the following forks of Bitcoin is focused on improving privacy features?

    ☐ Bitcoin Cash   ☐ Bitcoin Gold   ☐ Bitcoin Diamond   ☐ Bitcoin Private

9. What was the main reason for the creation of Bitcoin SV?

    ☐ To increase the maximum block size and allow for more transactions per block
    ☐ To decrease the maximum block size and make the network more decentralized
    ☐ To implement a new consensus algorithm to replace proof-of-work
    ☐ To restore the original Satoshi Vision of Bitcoin and increase the block size to 128MB

10. How does soft fork Taproot improve transaction privacy in the Bitcoin network?

    ☐ It encrypts transaction data using Diffie-Hellman key.
    ☐ It combines multiple transactions into a single transaction, obfuscating individual inputs and outputs.
    ☐ It allows users to create stealth addresses, making it difficult to link transactions to specific addresses.
    ☐ It introduces confidential transactions, where the transaction amounts are hidden.

Chapter 8 — Break Me (Bitcoin) if You Can

Bitcoin is Non-Governed

Bitcoin runs on rules without any rulers. It is non-governed unlike any other financial model.

- Not controlled by Miners
- Not controlled by Developers
- Not controlled by any Entity
- There is not even a voting governance.

51% Attack

If a miner controls majority of the hashrate, there can be "51% Attack" to double-spend.

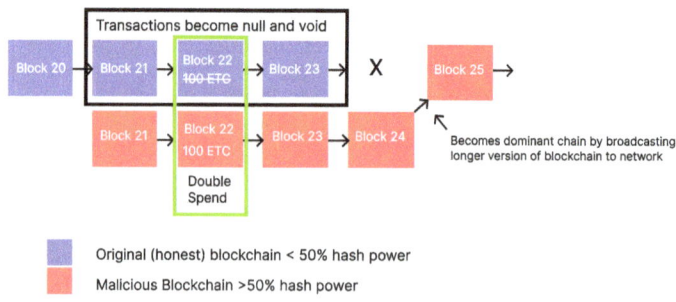

Controlling more than 50% hash rate, they can change the record of the block. Such attacks are costly in terms of energy required to continuously control the hash rate as honest nodes catches up.

Such attacker can only double-spend their own BTC.

Breaking SHA256 w/ Quantum Computing

1. Quantum computer with 1.9 billion qubits could essentially crack the encryption safeguarding Bitcoin within a mere 10 minutes.

2. IBM unveiled its 127-qubit processor just last year, while a unit sporting 1,000 qubits is set to be completed by the end of 2023

Quantum attack can happen in distant future. It will affect not only bitcoin, but all banking system. Hence, quantum attack resistant cryptography solution will be patched.

Exploit/Error in Bitcoin Code

Bitcoin's uptime is 99.988%. Since it's inception, bitcoin is down for only 14 hours 47 minutes.

- CVE-2010-5139: Bitcoin's Value Overflow Incident (Exploited) - 8 hours and 27 minutes of downtime
- CVE-2013-3220: Bitcoin's Migration From BerkeleyDB to LevelDB Incident (Exploited)
  - 6 hours and 20 minutes of downtime

> **Link to Explore**
> - https://en.bitcoin.it/wiki/Common_Vulnerabilities_and_Exposures

Total Shut-down for Electric Outage

Electric Outage can shut down Bitcoin network, but can traditional financial system survive shut down?

Link to Explore
- https://en.wikipedia.org/wiki/List_of_major_power_outages

Hacks & Thefts

Bitcoin has remained secure despite multiple instances of hacks targeting wallets, exchanges, and bridges.

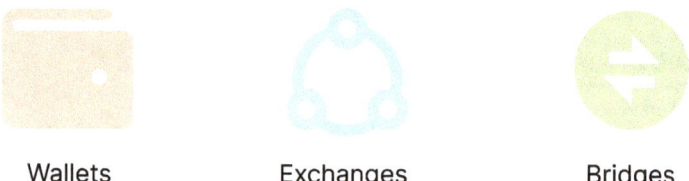

Wallets   Exchanges   Bridges

Governmental Bans

What if all countries ban? Can all countries unite against Bitcoin?

Link to Explore
- https://en.wikipedia.org/wiki/Legality_of_cryptocurrency_by_country_or_territory

Activity

Choose the correct answer below.

1. What is a bug in Bitcoin software?

- [ ] An error or flaw in the code that can cause unexpected behavior or vulnerabilities
- [ ] A type of Bitcoin transaction
- [ ] A security feature that protects Bitcoin users
- [ ] Flies found in Bitcoin ATM

2. How can quantum computing pose a threat to Bitcoin security?

- [ ] By allowing attackers to crack the cryptographic algorithms that secure Bitcoin
- [ ] By increasing the number of transactions on the network, leading to congestion and delays
- [ ] By exposing users' private keys to potential theft or loss
- [ ] None of the above

3. What was the impact of the ValueOverflow bug in 2018 on the Bitcoin network?

- [ ] It allowed attackers to create new Bitcoin out of thin air
- [ ] It caused delays and congestion on the Bitcoin network
- [ ] It had no impact on the Bitcoin network
- [ ] It was never exploited

4. What was the first major bug in Bitcoin's history?

- [ ] The SegWit2x bug
- [ ] The Heartbleed bug
- [ ] The transaction malleability bug
- [ ] The inflation bug

Break me (Bitcoin) if you can

> **Activity**

5. What did the inflation bug allow?

   ☐ Miners to create more Bitcoin than intended by the protocol
   ☐ Users to double-spend their Bitcoin
   ☐ Hackers to steal Bitcoin from exchanges
   ☐ None of the above

6. What did the transaction malleability bug allow?

   ☐ Users to double-spend their Bitcoin
   ☐ Hackers to steal Bitcoin from exchanges
   ☐ Miners to manipulate transaction data
   ☐ None of the above

7. What was the impact of the Heartbleed bug on the Bitcoin network?

   ☐ It allowed attackers to steal private keys and user funds from Bitcoin exchanges
   ☐ It had no impact on the Bitcoin network
   ☐ It caused delays and congestion on the Bitcoin network
   ☐ None of the above

8. What was the impact of the SegWit2x bug on the Bitcoin network?

   ☐ It caused delays and congestion on the Bitcoin network
   ☐ It allowed attackers to double-spend Bitcoin
   ☐ It had no impact on the Bitcoin network
   ☐ None of the above

Activity

9. What is a potential solution to the threat of quantum computing on Bitcoin?

   ☐ Implementing quantum-resistant cryptographic algorithms
   ☐ Increasing the block size to accommodate more transactions
   ☐ Creating a new cryptocurrency that is not vulnerable to quantum computing
   ☐ None of the above

10. What is the risk of storing your Bitcoin on a centralized exchange?

    ☐ The exchange may be hacked or compromised, leading to theft of your Bitcoin
    ☐ The exchange may impose unnecessary fees or restrictions on your Bitcoin transactions
    ☐ The exchange may not properly validate your transactions, leading to lost funds
    ☐ All of the above

11. What is a potential solution to the risk of storing Bitcoin on a centralized exchange?

    ☐ Using a decentralized exchange that does not require custody of your Bitcoin
    ☐ Storing your Bitcoin in a hardware wallet that you control
    ☐ Using a multi-signature setup that requires multiple signatures to authorize transactions
    ☐ All of the above

12. What is the risk of an internet outage for Bitcoin users?

    ☐ Bitcoin transactions may not be able to be processed or validated
    ☐ Bitcoin miners may not be able to create new blocks on the blockchain
    ☐ Bitcoin users may not be able to access their Bitcoin or make transactions
    ☐ All of the above

Activity

13. What is a potential solution to the risk of an internet outage for Bitcoin users?

    ☐ Using a satellite-based Bitcoin node or transaction relay service
    ☐ Using a mesh network to create a decentralized and resilient internet connection
    ☐ Having backup internet connections and power sources
    ☐ All of the above

14. What is 51% attack?

    ☐ A type of Bitcoin transaction that requires 51% consensus from the network
    ☐ A hacker gaining control of 51% or more of the mining power on the Bitcoin network
    ☐ A bug in the Bitcoin software that allows attackers to bypass security measures
    ☐ None of the above

15. Who controls bitcoin?

    ☐ Miners ☐ Nodes ☐ Developers ☐ Rules

Break me (Bitcoin) if you can

Chapter 9 — Scaling Into the Future

Layers: 0, 1, 2, 3

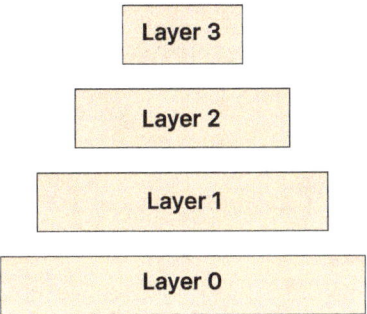

- 0: provides the basic services for consensus mechanisms, networking and applications. Example: Cosmos.

- 1: deals with data management, networking, execution of transactions. Example: Bitcoin, Ethereum.

- 2: improves the performance and scalability of layer 1. Example: Lightning Network, Polygon, Optimism

- 3: decentralized applications. Examples: DeFi dApps

Bitcoin Scalability Parameters

- 10 minutes of BlockTime
- 1 mb BlockSize (4 mb BlockWeight)
- 3-7 TPS

Layer 2 of Bitcoin: Lightning Network

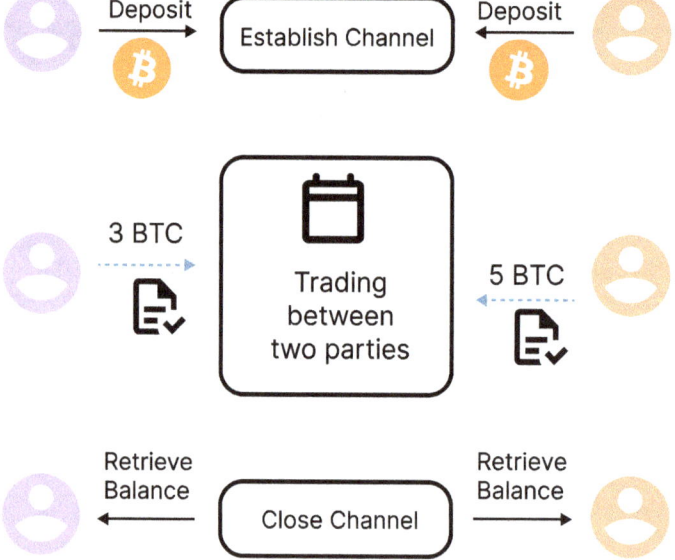

To understand Lightning Network, consider an example of restaurant. You can order multiple times and only settle payment when you leave.

In Lightning network of bitcoin, the first transaction is on-chain to set up a channel. Then two parties can transact multiple times off-chain (TPS goes a million txns per second) with little to no cost.

At closing channel, final settlement transaction happens on-chain. That's how Lightning Network works saving transaction fees and processing time.

Layer 2 of Bitcoin: Sidechain

Sidechain:

- Liquid Network: For traders and exchanges
- Stacks: For smart contract, DeFi and NFTs, DEXes
- DEXes: ALEX labs

Sidechains operates parallel to the main Bitcoin blockchain using a "two-way peg" mechanism, which enables assets to be securely transferred between the Bitcoin blockchain and the sidechain.

This ensures that assets moved to the sidechain can be redeemed and returned to the Bitcoin blockchain when needed.

Layer 2 of Bitcoin: Smart Contracts

Taproot and Bitcoin Smart Contracts

- Pay to Public Key Hash (P2PKH) + Multisig + Time locked
- Pay to Script Hash (P2SH): SegWit
- Pay to Taproot (P2TR): P2TR uses <u>Merkelized Alternative Script Trees (MAST)</u> to allow bitcoin to be sent to up to 2^128 different, arbitrary scripts.

Link to Explore

- https://www.youtube.com/watch?v=yU3Sr07Qnxg&ab_channel=SFBitcoinDevelopers

Taproot was activated through a soft fork in 2021. Taproot enables more complex and expressive smart contracts by introducing a new scripting language called "Tapscript."

Layer 2 of Bitcoin: Assets

Taro Protocol:

- Taproot Asset Representation Overlay
- Assets issuance on top of Bitcoin

Ordinals & Runes

Ordinals & Runes are two protocols developed by Casey Rodarmor.

Ordinals allows for NFT-like "inscriptions" on the Bitcoin network, whereas Runes focuses on fungible tokens, similar to BRC20.

Layer 3 of Bitcoin

- Bitcoin DeFi: The ALEX Lab Foundation, SVM, Bridges, Botanix Labs
- Bitcoin NFTs: Ordinals
  Inscriptions – NFTs (Jpegs or any media file but mostly Jpegs)
- UniSat, Ordinals Wallet

BRC-20, ORC-20, SRC-20, Runes vs Ordinals

- BRC-20 Tokens (Fixed supply meme coins)
- ORC-20 Tokens (Flexible supply meme coins)
- SRC-20 Tokens/Stamps (Tokens and Tokenised offerings of NFTs)

Activity

Choose the correct answer below.

1. **What is the purpose of Bitcoin's layer 2 solution?**

   ☐ To increase transaction speed and reduce fees
   ☐ To add new features to the Bitcoin protocol
   ☐ To improve security on the Bitcoin network
   ☐ To allow for more efficient mining of Bitcoin blocks

2. **What is the Lightning Network?**

   ☐ A hardware wallet used for storing Bitcoin
   ☐ A hard fork of Bitcoin that introduced new features
   ☐ Layer 2 that allows for faster and cheaper Bitcoin transactions
   ☐ An anonymous messaging platform built on top of the Bitcoin protocol

3. **What is SegWit?**

   ☐ A scaling solution that separates transaction data from signature data
   ☐ A consensus algorithm used by Bitcoin miners
   ☐ A privacy-focused Bitcoin wallet
   ☐ An alternative cryptocurrency to Bitcoin

4. **What is Taproot?**

   ☐ A protocol used to prevent double-spending attacks
   ☐ A lightning-fast payment network built on top of Bitcoin
   ☐ A Bitcoin mining pool
   ☐ A soft fork that adds new transaction types and improves privacy

Activity

5. What is a sidechain?

- [ ] An independent blockchain that is attached to the Bitcoin network
- [ ] A type of Bitcoin transaction that uses fewer data
- [ ] A security feature that protects against 51% attacks
- [ ] A type of wallet used to store Bitcoin on mobile devices

6. Which of the following is a benefit of using a sidechain?

- [ ] Increased transaction speed
- [ ] Improved privacy
- [ ] Lower transaction fees
- [ ] All of the above

7. What is the function of Watchtowers in Lightning?

- [ ] To settle lightning payments
- [ ] To monitor the network for any attempts of fraud by keeping an eye on the network
- [ ] To provide lightning-fast transactions
- [ ] To act as a decentralized exchange for cryptocurrencies

8. Which of the following is a disadvantage of using the Lightning Network?

- [ ] Higher transaction fees
- [ ] Slower transaction speed
- [ ] Requires constant internet connectivity
- [ ] None of the above

Activity

9. What is the purpose of the Taproot upgrade?
   - [ ] To improve Bitcoin's scalability
   - [ ] To improve Bitcoin's privacy and security
   - [ ] To create a new type of cryptocurrency
   - [ ] To replace the proof-of-work consensus algorithm

10. Who created Ordinals Theory in Bitcoin for NFTs?
    - [ ] Casey Rodarmor
    - [ ] Domo
    - [ ] Udi
    - [ ] Adam Back

11. What is the name of the first NFT that was created on the Bitcoin network?
    - [ ] CryptoPunks
    - [ ] CryptoKitties
    - [ ] Rare Pepe
    - [ ] Decentraland

Chapter 10 — How To Acquire Bitcoin

Buy Bitcoin (4 ways)

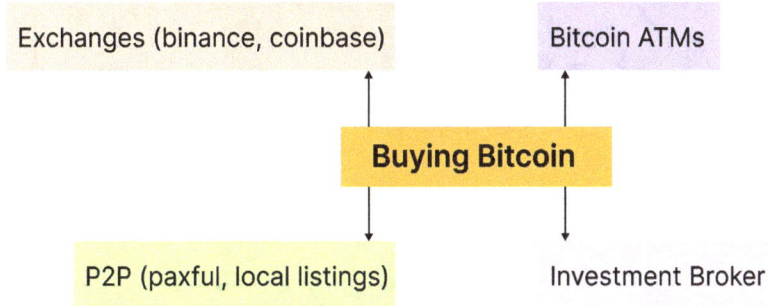

Earn Bitcoin (12 ways)

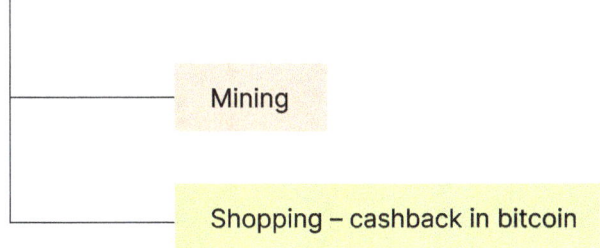

- Job compensation in bitcoin
- Bounty Hunting
- Referrals
- Airdrops converted in bitcoin
- X-to-Earn (Play games, Watch ads, Exercises, Quizzes)
- Trading
- Staking
- Lending-borrowing

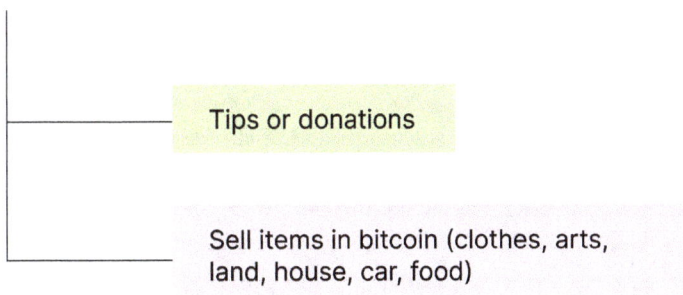

Pre-requisites

There are few prerequisites we must have before acquiring bitcoin:

- Create and Maintain Wallets
- Safety Measures of Seed Phrase or Private Key
- Knowledge to Avoid Phishing Sites or Scams

Activity

Choose the correct answer below.

1. What is the process of solving complex mathematical equations to verify Bitcoin transactions and adding them to the blockchain called?

   ☐ Mining   ☐ Trading   ☐ Staking   ☐ Lending

2. Which of the following is NOT a way to earn Bitcoin?

   ☐ Mining   ☐ Trading   ☐ Hacking   ☐ Faucets

3. What is a Bitcoin faucet?

   ☐ A physical device used for Bitcoin mining
   ☐ A website or app that gives away small amounts of Bitcoin for completing tasks
   ☐ A marketplace for trading Bitcoin
   ☐ A type of Bitcoin wallet

4. How can you acquire Bitcoin through peer-to-peer (P2P) trading?

   ☐ Mining
   ☐ Coinbase
   ☐ Wallets
   ☐ Paxful

5. What is a Bitcoin ATM?

   ☐ A machine that takes fiat & transfers Bitcoin
   ☐ A machine that mines Bitcoin
   ☐ A hardware wallet for storing Bitcoin
   ☐ A type of Bitcoin exchange

Activity

6. What type of wallet is recommended for storing Bitcoin long-term?

    ☐ Paper Wallet   ☐ Hardware Wallet   ☐ Mobile Wallet   ☐ Desktop Wallet

7. Which of the following is a common mistake that Bitcoin beginners make?

    ☐ Using a weak password for their Bitcoin wallet
    ☐ Sending Bitcoin to the wrong address
    ☐ Falling for a Bitcoin scam
    ☐ All of the above

8. What is a Bitcoin exchange?

    ☐ A website or app that allows users to buy, sell, and trade Bitcoin
    ☐ A physical location where Bitcoin can be acquired
    ☐ A process of earning Bitcoin by lending it to others
    ☐ A type of Bitcoin wallet

9. What is the term used for earning interest or rewards by giving your Bitcoin to others?

    ☐ Mining   ☐ Staking   ☐ Lending   ☐ Flash Loan

10. What is a private key in the context of acquiring Bitcoin?

    ☐ A password used to access a Bitcoin wallet
    ☐ A type of hardware used for Bitcoin mining
    ☐ A type of Bitcoin exchange
    ☐ A process of earning Bitcoin by lending it to others

Chapter 11 — Price of 1 Bitcoin

Where Does The Price Come From?

Value of bitcoin comes from the ability to embed transaction messages in a globally distributed and timestamped immutable database.

This value determines the price of bitcoin through 3 channels.

Supply & Demand
(Human Psychology)

Market Making
(Business)

Manipulation
(news, policies, events)

Production Cost

Electricity Cost in Nepal	$0.11/kWh
• Electricity to mine 1 BTC	• 427,272 kW
• 1 BTC Mining Power Cost	• $47000

As per 2025

Trading Market: Buy & Sell

- Spot trading exchanges
- Derivatives
- Futures & Margins

Stock-to-Flow Theory (S2F)

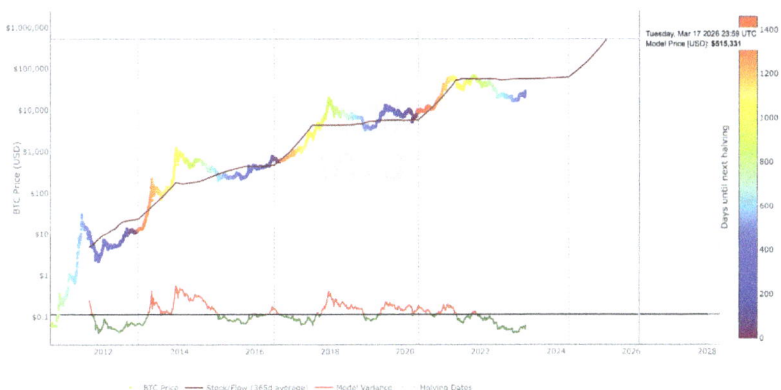

S2F model was developed by pseudonymous analyst Plan B in 2019. Based on scarcity, this model tries to find years of production to get current bitcoin supply.

S2F correctly predicted price of bitcoin after 2020 halving to reach $55k average.

> **Link to Explore**
> - https://www.lookintobitcoin.com/charts/stock-to-flow-model/

Predictions: All-in vs Nothing

- Hyperinflation of fiats
- Banking failures
- Bitcoin's value is binary: either [0] or [Global Money]

Intrinsic Value

Fiat currencies: Physical/Digital, Government, Politics, Infinite Supply

Gold: Physical, Ornaments, Jewelry, Fashion, Unknown Supply

Bitcoin: Digital, Cryptography, Proof-of-work, Deterministic Supply

Which one has intrinsic value?

Price of 1 Bitcoin

Activity

Choose the correct answer below.

1. What gives Bitcoin its value?

   ☐ Its scarcity ☐ Its utility ☐ Its legal status ☐ Its price history

2. How is the value of Bitcoin determined?

   ☐ Through supply and demand
   ☐ Through government regulations
   ☐ Through mining difficulty
   ☐ Through technological advancements

3. What is the maximum supply of Bitcoin?

   ☐ 10 million ☐ 21 million ☐ 50 million ☐ 100 million

4. What is the S2F value of Bitcoin at halving of 2024?

   ☐ 119.86 ☐ 55.94 ☐ Undefined ☐ 503.42

5. It is possible to predict the price of bitcoin. True or false?

   ☐ True ☐ False

6. How has the value of Bitcoin changed over time?

   ☐ It has steadily increased
   ☐ It has steadily decreased
   ☐ It has been volatile
   ☐ It has remained stable

Activity

7. What are some factors that can influence the value of Bitcoin?

   ☐ News events
   ☐ Government regulations
   ☐ Market sentiment
   ☐ All of the above

8. How does the value of Bitcoin compare to traditional assets like gold or stocks?

   ☐ It is more volatile
   ☐ It is less volatile
   ☐ It has similar volatility
   ☐ Its volatility depends on market conditions

9. What is the significance of Bitcoin?

   ☐ It is the world's first decentralized digital currency
   ☐ It has revolutionized the financial industry
   ☐ It is a store of value
   ☐ All of the above

10. How is the value of Bitcoin affected by its adoption rate?

    ☐ The more widely it is adopted, the higher its value
    ☐ The more widely it is adopted, the lower its value
    ☐ Adoption rate has no impact on its value
    ☐ Adoption rate only affects short-term fluctuations

Price of 1 Bitcoin

Chapter 12 — Wallets vs Banks

Where Are the Bitcoins?

- Not in wallets
- Not in someone's account
- Always in the Bitcoin Network

Wallets

- Access to bitcoins is through private keys (public keys)
- Private/Public keys are managed through "Wallets"
- Proves the ownership of crypto

Features of Wallet

Manage Public/Private Keys	Send/Transfer/Spend Crypto	Receive Crypto
Browse dApps	Proof of Ownership	Sign message

Types of Wallet

Categories:
- Non-custodial [Private Key access] [Ledger, Exodus, Blue]
- Custodial [No Private Key access] [Exchanges Wallet]

Types:

 **Cold Wallet :** [Private Key Not Exposed To Internet] [Hardware Wallet: Ledger, Trezor]

 Hot Wallet : Hot Wallet [Private Key Exposed To Internet] [Software Wallet: Metamask]

 Paper Wallet : Paper Wallet [Private Key Not Exposed To Internet] [Paper]

Wallet vs Bank

- Banks or Bank Accounts hold your money, control your money for you.
- Banks and banking services are middlemen doing their business.
- Wallet is making individuals themselves a bank.
- With Wallet, you hold or control your money yourself.

> Activity

Choose the correct answer below.

1. Which of the following is a key difference between Bitcoin wallets and bank accounts?
   - [ ] Bitcoin wallets are physical devices, while bank accounts are digital
   - [ ] Bitcoin wallets are anonymous, while bank accounts require personal identification
   - [ ] Bitcoin wallets are regulated by governments, while bank accounts are not
   - [ ] Bitcoin wallets do not require passwords, while bank accounts do

2. What is the primary purpose of a Bitcoin wallet?
   - [ ] To store physical Bitcoins
   - [ ] To mine Bitcoins
   - [ ] To facilitate Bitcoin transactions
   - [ ] To earn interest on Bitcoins

3. Which of the following is a disadvantage of using a Bitcoin wallet compared to a bank account?
   - [ ] Bitcoin wallets offer higher interest rates
   - [ ] Bitcoin wallets have lower fees for transactions
   - [ ] Bitcoin wallets are not insured by FDIC
   - [ ] Bitcoin wallets provide better customer service

4. Which of the following is a key feature of a hardware Bitcoin wallet?
   - [ ] It is an online wallet
   - [ ] It requires an internet connection to access
   - [ ] It stores private keys offline
   - [ ] It is free to use

Activity

5. What is the level of control over funds in a Bitcoin wallet compared to a bank account?

   ☐ Users have more control over their funds in a Bitcoin wallet
   ☐ Users have less control over their funds in a Bitcoin wallet
   ☐ Users have the same level of control over their funds in a Bitcoin wallet as in a bank account
   ☐ Bitcoin wallets do not provide any control over funds

6. Which of the following is a feature of a bank account that is not available in most Bitcoin wallets?

   ☐ Transaction privacy
   ☐ Customer Service Support
   ☐ Lower transaction fees
   ☐ Faster transaction times

7. How are transaction fees typically calculated in a Bitcoin wallet compared to a bank account?

   ☐ Transaction fees in a Bitcoin wallet are fixed, while bank account transaction fees are variable
   ☐ Transaction fees in a Bitcoin wallet do not depend on transaction amount, while bank account transaction fees depend on transaction amount.
   ☐ Transaction fees in a Bitcoin wallet are higher, while bank account transaction fees are lower
   ☐ Transaction fees in a Bitcoin wallet are lower, while bank account transaction fees are higher

Activity

8. What is the main advantage of using a multi-signature Bitcoin wallet?

   ☐ It is the most convenient type of wallet
   ☐ It offers the highest level of security
   ☐ It does not require any passwords
   ☐ It has the lowest transaction fees

9. Which of the following is NOT a risk associated with using a Bitcoin wallet compared to a bank account?

   ☐ Higher volatility of the asset
   ☐ Potential for hacking or cyberattacks
   ☐ Limited acceptance by merchants
   ☐ Inability to make international transactions

10. Which of the following is a characteristic of a Bitcoin wallet compared to a bank account in terms of accessibility?

    ☐ Bitcoin wallet can be accessed 24/7 without any restrictions
    ☐ Bank account can be accessed 24/7 without any restrictions
    ☐ Both Bitcoin wallet and bank account have limited access hours
    ☐ Neither Bitcoin wallet nor bank account can be accessed on weekends.

Chapter 13 — Apolitical Manifesto

Core Values of Bitcoin

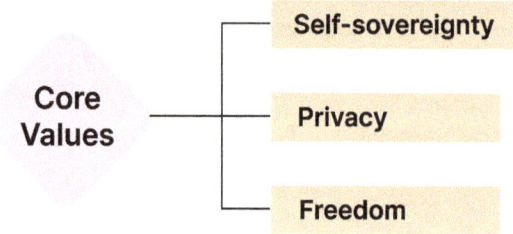

But People are Political

- Bitcoin supporters seem to come from libertarian political view
- Bitcoin non-supporter, Warren Buffet, says Bitcoin is a rat poison
- Michael Saylor says Bitcoin is the only future
- Political candidates now bring Bitcoin in their agendas

Bitcoin Does Not Care Who You Are

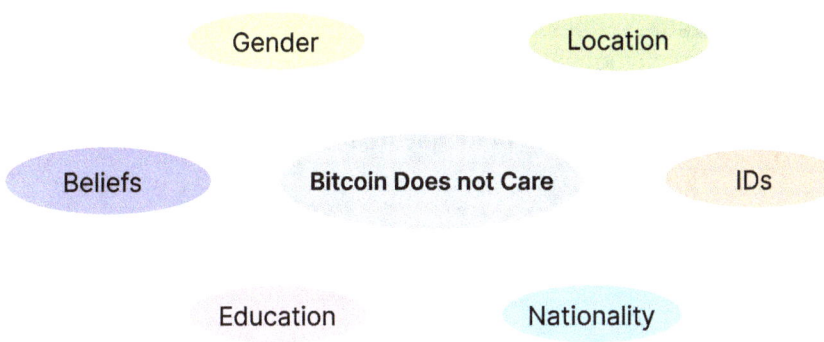

- User needs just the sufficient miner fee to do transaction. That's all.

Governance of Bitcoin

- **Governance by infrastructure:**
  Bitcoin's law is ruled by code.

- **Governance of infrastructure:**
  Bitcoin's code is maintained by few people that goes through rigorous discussion and audits from the community.

Bitcoin Ideology

- **Deflationary world:** Limited supply || Impact on buyer/seller
- **Distributed Capitalism:** Everyone can participate but over-accumulation motivated
- **Failure of credit system:** Exiting from debt based economy
- **Libertarian:** Separation of money from states

Activity

Choose the correct answer below.

1. What is the meaning of Bitcoin's apolitical nature?
- [ ] It is not affiliated with any political party
- [ ] It is not influenced by political decisions or agendas
- [ ] It is against political activism
- [ ] It promotes political neutrality

2. How does Bitcoin's apolitical nature benefit its users?
- [ ] It provides a more stable and secure financial system
- [ ] It allows for greater privacy and anonymity in financial transactions
- [ ] It eliminates the risk of government interference or seizure of funds
- [ ] All of the above

3. What is the relationship between Bitcoin and traditional political systems?
- [ ] Bitcoin is in opposition to traditional political systems
- [ ] Bitcoin can coexist with traditional political systems
- [ ] Bitcoin seeks to replace traditional political systems
- [ ] Bitcoin has no relationship with traditional political systems

4. How does Bitcoin's apolitical nature impact its price?
- [ ] It makes it more volatile
- [ ] It makes it less volatile
- [ ] It has no impact on price volatility
- [ ] It only impacts short-term price fluctuations

Activity

5. What is the stance of Bitcoin on social issues?

   ☐ It takes no stance on social issues
   ☐ It promotes social activism and change
   ☐ It is actively opposed to social justice movements
   ☐ It supports social justice movements but does not get involved in political activism

6. What is the economic philosophy behind Bitcoin?

   ☐ Keynesianism   ☐ Marxism   ☐ Austrian economics   ☐ Neo-classical economics

7. Which ideology is closer to Bitcoin?

   ☐ Libertarianism   ☐ Socialism   ☐ Conservatism   ☐ Capitalism

8. What is the role of government in Bitcoin's philosophy?

   ☐ Government should be limited in its power and control over the economy
   ☐ Government should have a strong role in regulating the economy
   ☐ Government should be replaced with market forces
   ☐ Government should have no role in regulating the economy

9. What is the view of Bitcoin's philosophy on individual privacy?

   ☐ It supports government surveillance in the interest of national security
   ☐ It advocates for strong protection of individual privacy
   ☐ It seeks to eliminate privacy entirely
   ☐ It has no stance on individual privacy

Activity

10. How does Bitcoin's philosophy view individual property rights?
- [ ] It opposes individual property rights in favor of communal ownership
- [ ] It has no stance on individual property rights
- [ ] It seeks to eliminate property rights entirely
- [ ] It advocates for strong protection of individual property rights

Chapter 14 — Financial Freedom

The World We Live In

- **1.7B** : Adults are unbanked
- **1B** : People live on poverty (less than $1.90 per day)
- **4.7b** : People have mobile phones

- **50%** : Population of Nepal is unbanked
- **29%** : Population of Nepal is poor
- **65%** : Population of Nepal has access to mobile phones

The Way We Live In

- Our lives are entangled with:

    Level 1: food, housing, clothes, security, health, education
    Level 2: family, relationships, jobs, status
    Level 3: freedom, growth, recognition, awakening

- More than 99% people live within Level 1 & Level 2 – impacted 100% by money (wealth).

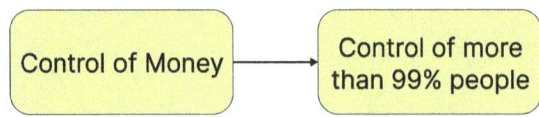

That's why government controls money to control our lives.

Financial Freedom

What Happened In 1971?

- ◇ President Richard Nixon ended the Bretton Woods financial system → this untied the exchange value of US dollar to gold.
- ◇ Since 1971, productivity increased while wages stagnated, GDP rose, but workers' share declined, and house prices soared
- ◇ Hyperinflation started, currencies crashed, banking crises happened. Economic inequality widened.
- ◇ Positives: Increased life expectancy, improved infant survival rates, decline in global poverty rates and technological progress

Why Nixon killed Bretton Woods financial system?

The government ran into trouble backing the currency with gold in the late 1960s, after printing too much money to pay the Vietnam War and various welfare programs.

1971 marks the end of Gold Standard.

Central banks now possess the unprecedented ability to create an unlimited supply of their respective currencies at will.

Fix The Money, Fix The World

of Wealth is controlled by 1% of People (close to governments)

Corruption, Crimes, Inflation & Wars – funded by "money printing" mostly in cash

Fiats backed by governments & banks are non-transparent, non-traceable, and non-accountable.

People closer to governments and banks are 1st beneficiaries than rest of the world in fiat system.

We need sound money, hard money. **#Bitcoin**
We need money "not" controlled by anyone. **#Bitcoin**
We need money that makes corruption, crimes, & wars unaffordable. **#Bitcoin**

Paths To Freedom

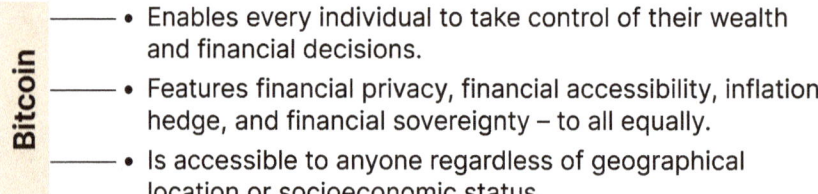

Financial Freedom

Is Freedom The Need?

- **Hungary: August 1945** | Highest monthly inflation rate: 4.19 × 10^16% | Reason: War

- **Yugoslavia: April 1992** | Highest monthly inflation rate: 313,000,000% | Reason: Politics

- **Zimbabwe: March 2007** | Highest monthly inflation rate: 7.96 × 10^10% | Reason: Government Policies

- **Venezuela: Jan 2019** | Highest monthly inflation rate: 2.68 × 10^6 % | Reason: Government Policies

- Let's ask the importance of Bitcoin to people of Turkey, people of Argentina, people of Sri Lanka, people of Pakistan.

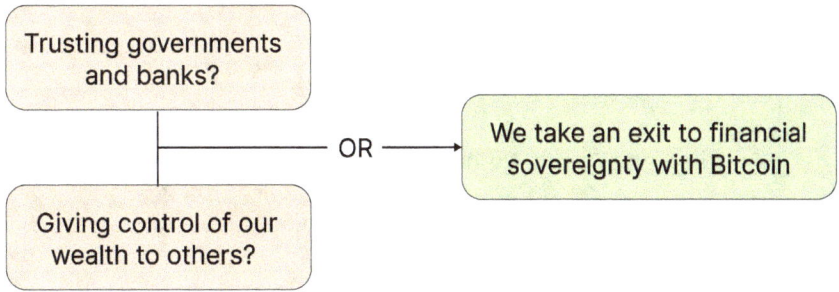

Banking the Unbanked

- ◇ Bitcoin provides access to financial services for the unbanked to send and receive money.
- ◇ Cost-effective, available 24/7/365
- ◇ Access to global economy for everyone, borderless.
- ◇ On September 7, 2021, El Salvador became the first country to officially adopt bitcoin as legal tender.

Bitcoin In A Life of An Individual

- → **Taihuttu family:** a case study of Dutch family for their decision to sell their possessions and invest in Bitcoin in 2016. Still going fine on 2025.

- → **Bitcoin Nomad:** Surviving with only Bitcoin

- → **Imagine having your wealth in Bitcoin vs Others** – Now imagine the worst cases: Civil war, Earthquake, Flood, Government Failure, Alien invasion.

Activity

Choose the correct answer below.

1. Which currency is considered more volatile in terms of value fluctuations?

   ☐ Bitcoin   ☐ Yen   ☐ USD   ☐ Euro

2. Which form of currency is decentralized and not controlled by any central authority?

   ☐ Gold   ☐ Stocks   ☐ Bitcoin   ☐ Bonds

3. Which form of currency provides more privacy and security in transactions?

   ☐ Rai Stones   ☐ Fiat money   ☐ Real Estates   ☐ Bitcoin

4. Which currency is not influenced by government policies or economic conditions of a country?

   ☐ Bitcoin
   ☐ Fiat money
   ☐ Both are influenced by government policies
   ☐ None of the above

5. Which form of currency has limited supply, with a maximum cap on the total number of units that can be created?

   ☐ Ethereum   ☐ Fiat money   ☐ Gold   ☐ Bitcoin

6. Which currency has lower transaction fees for international transfers?

   ☐ Fiat money   ☐ Bitcoin   ☐ Gold   ☐ MoneyGram

Activity

7. Which currency can be used for cross-border transactions without the need for intermediaries?

   ☐ Bitcoin   ☐ US Dollars   ☐ Both require intermediaries   ☐ Apple Stocks

8. Which currency has higher potential for store of value ?

   ☐ Bitcoin
   ☐ Fiat money
   ☐ Both have equal potential for store of value
   ☐ None of the above

9. Which form of currency is more resistant to inflation and currency devaluation?

   ☐ Chinese Yen   ☐ Fiat money   ☐ Both are equally resistant   ☐ Bitcoin

10. Which form of currency requires greater technological literacy for transactions?

    ☐ Gold   ☐ Fiat money   ☐ Bitcoin   ☐ None of the above

Chapter 15 — Inheritance Planning

SoV: Generation to Generations

- We care: future of our kids. NO DOUBT.

- Before we die – we try to secure the future of our kids, we accumulate wealth, status and reputation to pass on.
- Physical assets = Easy to hand over to future generations
- But Bitcoin is 100% digital asset that advocates store of value (SoV) through self-custody.

Problems of Self-Custody

- Self-custody = Ownership control. Imagine you accumulated Bitcoin, only to lose it forever with your death.
- If you die unexpectedly, how do you make sure your family or kids receive "self-custodied" wealth like Bitcoin.
- With great power (financial freedom), comes great responsibility (inheritance planning).
- Bitcoins are accessed through private key and recovered through seed phrases. Private key and seed phrases are not to be revealed to anyone except the owner. How do you hand over such assets then?

Too Much Has Been Lost

3.8 M BTC LOST
3.8 million Bitcoins (approximately 20% of the total supply) are lost forever, with reasons including - lost private keys, - forgotten passwords, and - wallet corruption.

Hard Drive Disposal
James Howell's Hard Drive Disposal: threw away an old hard drive that had a digital wallet containing 7,500 bitcoins

Forgotten Password
Stefan Thomas' Forgotten Password: lost around 7,000 bitcoins due to a forgotten password

Wallet Failure
Mark Frauenfelder's Trezor Wallet Failure: lost bitcoin as recovery seed was unreadable due to ink fading

2 Keys of Inheritance Planning

- **Technical Planning:**
  Managing private keys, seed phrases, wallets

- **Legal Planning:**
  Wills, Power of attorney, Taxes

Importance of Inheritance Planning

- Bitcoins are intangible digital assets not governed by traditional inheritance laws
- Without a proper inheritance plan, bitcoin may be lost, inaccessible, or transferred to unintended beneficiaries, resulting in potential financial losses and legal disputes.
- Planning for the transfer of bitcoin can also help individuals maintain control over their digital assets and ensure that their wishes are respected after their death.

Existing Solutions

1. Backup seed phrases or private keys
2. Bitcoin time lock contract/script
3. Naming beneficiaries in someone's will or estate plans
4. Establishing trust (revocable and irrevocable)
5. Multi-sig wallet management
6. Sovrin Project (with Decentralized Identities - DID)
7. In these solutions, there are 2 ways: - Either storing private key or seed phrases somewhere safe with legal bind. - Or storing funds in smart contracts with conditions for digital identities of beneficiaries

Potential Solutions

- Transfer on Death (TOD) smart contract:

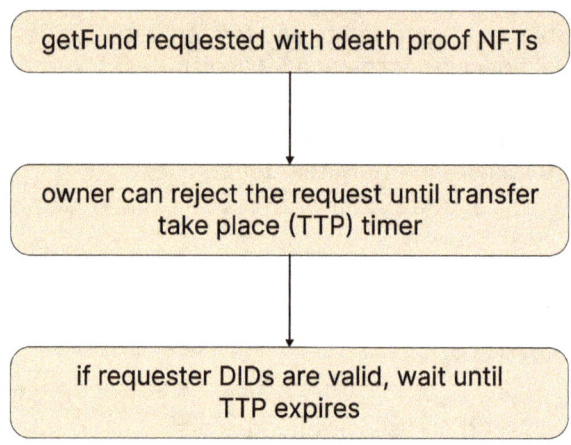

> **Link to Explore**
>
> - https://papers.ssrn.com/sol3/papers.cfm?abstract_id=4183803

> Activity

Choose the correct answer below.

1. What is crypto inheritance planning?

☐ Planning for the transfer of cryptocurrencies after death or incapacity
☐ Planning for the creation of new cryptocurrencies
☐ Planning for the acquisition of cryptocurrencies through mining
☐ Planning for the regulation of cryptocurrencies by governments

2. Who lost 7,500 Bitcoins in garbage landfill?

☐ Stefan Thomas   ☐ Mark Frauenfelder   ☐ James Howell   ☐ Satoshi Nakamoto

3. What are some key considerations in crypto inheritance planning?

☐ Storing private keys securely
☐ Creating a will or trust that includes cryptocurrencies
☐ Appointing a trusted executor or trustee
☐ All of the above. Correct answer: d) All of the above

4. What happens to cryptocurrencies if the owner passes away without a crypto inheritance plan?

☐ Cryptocurrencies are automatically transferred to the government
☐ Cryptocurrencies are automatically transferred to the next of kin
☐ Cryptocurrencies become inaccessible and may be lost forever
☐ Cryptocurrencies are distributed to all users on the blockchain.

5. Which of the following is NOT a common method for transferring cryptocurrencies in a crypto inheritance plan?

☐ Adding cryptocurrencies to a will or trust
☐ Sharing private keys or wallet credentials with trusted individuals
☐ Registering cryptocurrencies with a government agency
☐ Using a multisig wallet that requires multiple signatures for transactions.

Activity

6. What is a private key?

   ☐ A secret code used to access a cryptocurrency
   ☐ A government-issued identification number for cryptocurrencies
   ☐ A public address for receiving cryptocurrencies
   ☐ A smart contract that governs the value of cryptocurrencies.

7. Which of the following is a potential risk in crypto inheritance planning?

   ☐ Loss of private keys or wallet credentials
   ☐ Hacking or cyberattacks on the cryptocurrency wallet
   ☐ Legal and regulatory changes affecting cryptocurrencies
   ☐ All of the above.

8. What is a multisig wallet?

   ☐ A wallet that allows multiple people to access and control cryptocurrencies
   ☐ A wallet that requires multiple signatures for every transaction
   ☐ A wallet that offers enhanced security features for protecting cryptocurrencies
   ☐ A wallet that can be used for mining multiple cryptocurrencies simultaneously.

9. What is the role of an executor or trustee in crypto inheritance planning?

   ☐ To create new cryptocurrencies on behalf of the deceased
   ☐ To distribute cryptocurrencies to beneficiaries according to the deceased's wishes
   ☐ To enforce government regulations on cryptocurrencies
   ☐ To transfer cryptocurrencies to charitable organizations.

Activity

10. What is a recovery seed phrase?

    ☐ A set of words used to recover a lost or forgotten private key
    ☐ A document that outlines the inheritance plan for cryptocurrencies
    ☐ A government-issued document for tracking cryptocurrencies
    ☐ A technical term for the raising seed money out of cryptocurrencies.

Chapter 16: Global Adoption vs Global Banning

Health of Bitcoin Network

Mining Hashrate:
819.17 Ehash/s

Active Address Growth:
694,508

Value Growth:
$12 to $108k in 13 y

Transaction Growth:
336,530 per day

Distribution

<1	1-10	10-100	100 – 1000	> 1000
7.01%	10.56%	21.75%	22.57%	38.11%

 Super Healthy Growth

-As per 2025

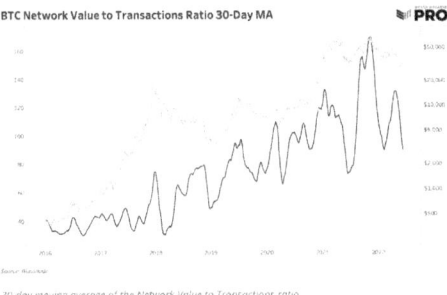

Source: Bitcoin Magazine Pro

Tracking the data from 2016, the growth of BTC network value is uptrend.

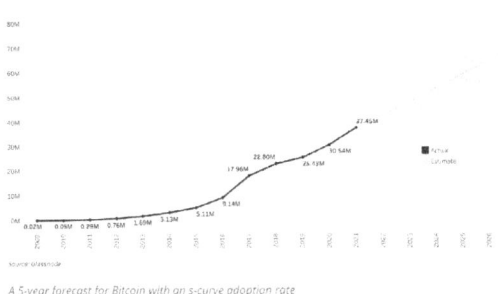

Based on s-curve adoption rate model, bitcoin will be used by 50 m within 2025 AD.

Year	Bitcoin Halving	Approximate Bitcoin Price at Halving
2012	1st Halving	$12
2016	2nd Halving	$650
2020	3rd Halving	$8,500
2024	4th Halving	$63,500

Who's Onboard?

- 2 country's legal tender (El Salvador, Central African Republic)

- 23 public companies (MicroStrategy Inc., Marathon Digital Holdings)

- Prominent People: Michael Saylor, Jack Dorsey, Adam Back, Tyler and Cameron Winklevoss, Michael Novogratz, Cynthia Lummis, Francis Suarez, Chamath Palihapitiya, Tim Draper, Raoul Pal.

Reason = Banking the Unbanked for Global Financial Freedom

Who's In Pain?

Central Banks & Bankers   Governments   Boomers (who loves physical goods)

- Warren Buffett, Charlie Munger, Nouriel Roubini, Peter Schiff, Jamie Dimon, Janet Yellen, Christine Lagarde

Reason = Less Power to Control Money to Control People's Lives.

Banning Also Triggers Adoption

- **Banning bitcoin promotes bitcoin aggressively.**
- P2P trades of bitcoin is growing rapidly in countries where bitcoin is banned or restricted.

Any news on Bitcoin: good or bad = Bitcoin reaches to more people

Ban vs Adoption: Who's Winning?

- Since inception 2009, Bitcoin survived with growth for continuous 14 years.
- Legal in 33 countries

- **Banned in 9 countries:**

   Algeria

   Bolivia

   Bangladesh

   Dominican Republic

   Ghana

  Nepal

  The Republic of Macedonia

   Qatar

  Vanuatu

- **Restricted in 7 countries:**

   Bahrain

   China

   Iran

   Kazakhstan

   Saudi Arabia

   Turkey

   Vietnam

Activity

Choose the correct answer below.

1. What is the current status of global "banning" and "adoption" of Bitcoin?
   - ☐ Bitcoin is globally banned and not accepted anywhere
   - ☐ Bitcoin is globally adopted and accepted everywhere
   - ☐ Bitcoin is banned in some countries and adopted in others
   - ☐ Bitcoin is banned in all countries except one

2. Which of the following countries has banned the trading of Bitcoin?
   - ☐ United States   ☐ Japan   ☐ Nepal   ☐ Germany

3. What is the main reason behind global banning of Bitcoin in some countries?
   - ☐ Concerns about illegal activities like money laundering
   - ☐ Lack of technological infrastructure to support Bitcoin
   - ☐ Fear of losing control over monetary policies
   - ☐ Religious beliefs

4. Which country has shown the highest level of adoption of Bitcoin as a legal tender?
   - ☐ El Salvador   ☐ United States   ☐ Australia   ☐ South Korea

5. What is the stance of major global central banks towards Bitcoin adoption?
   - ☐ Embracing Bitcoin as a mainstream currency
   - ☐ Banning Bitcoin in all their operations
   - ☐ Accepting Bitcoin as an investment tool only
   - ☐ Remaining neutral with no official stance

> **Activity**

6. Which of the following countries has a positive outlook towards Bitcoin adoption?

   ☐ United Kingdom ☐ Russia ☐ Brazil ☐ Saudi Arabia

7. How does global banning of Bitcoin impact its price and market value?

   ☐ Increases the price and market value
   ☐ Decreases the price and market value
   ☐ Does not impact the price and market value
   ☐ Results in extreme volatility in the price and market value

8. What are the main advantages of global adoption of Bitcoin?

   ☐ Faster and cheaper cross-border transactions
   ☐ Reduced dependency on traditional banking systems
   ☐ Increased financial inclusion for the unbanked population
   ☐ All of the above

9. What are the main challenges of global adoption of Bitcoin?

   ☐ Lack of regulatory framework and government support
   ☐ Volatility in the price of Bitcoin
   ☐ Security concerns and risks of cyberattacks
   ☐ All of the above

10. What is the most possible future outlook for global banning and adoption of Bitcoin?

    ☐ Bitcoin may be globally banned in all countries
    ☐ Bitcoin may be globally adopted as a mainstream currency
    ☐ Bitcoin may continue to grow facing a mixed response from countries
    ☐ Bitcoin may lose its relevance and fade away

Chapter 17 — Energy Debate

Origin of Burning Energy

- New monetary system "Bitcoin" needed fair distribution.
- Options: Airdrop, ICO, Premine, how?
- Satoshi decided a game plan similar to how gold is distributed.
- Gold miner input work – miner always need to sell it to cover costs
- Bitcoin miner input energy - miner always need to sell it to cover costs

Energy Integrated Money

- Proof-of-Work to make a valid block for
  1. BTC Issuance
  2. Processing/Settling transactions in real time

- Money originated & associated with work done (energy spent) without anyone's control vs Fiat Money originated & associated with only trust + control of government.

How Much Energy Does Bitcoin Consumes?

- 150 TerraWattHours per year (0.6% of Global usage)
- 50 Megatons of CO2 per year

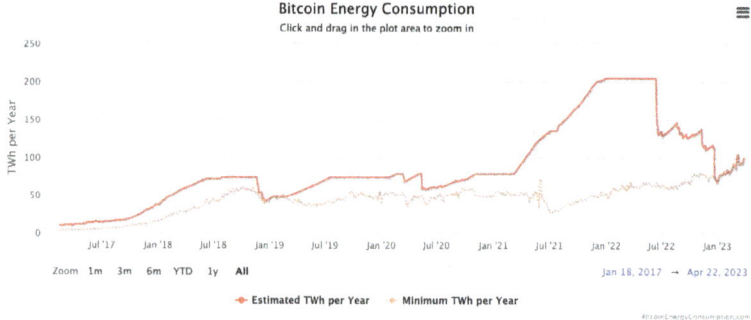

Source: bitcoinenergyconsumption.com

When bitcoin creates new ATH, more miners join the network for profit. This aligns with higher electric energy consumption in the chart.

Energy Debate

Compared to VISA

Electricity Energy Comparison	Carbon Footprint Comparison
607, 214	1,115,666
The number of VISA transactions that could be powered by the energy consumed for a single Bitcoin transaction on average (902.50 kWh).	The number of VISA transactions with a carbon footprint equal to the footprint of a single Bitcoin transaction (503.38 kgCO2) after factoring in the respective energy mix.

Compared To Gold

Gold Mining Footprint	Bitcoin Mining Footprint
11 tons CO2	158 tons CO2
The carbon footprint of one Bitcoin's worth of gold mined.	The carbon footprint of a single mined Bitcoin (inc. fees).

Compared to Banking System

- Banking system roughly used 4,981 TWh per year
- This make bitcoin 50 times energy efficient currently.
- Value settlement: $45 trillion per year (6% of global volume)

Bitcoin Electric Bill vs Income

Annualized Income	Ann. Electricity Costs	Cost Percentage
$10,059,527,186	$4,334,842,881	43.09%
Total value of mining rewards (including fees) per year.	Assuming a fixed rate of 5 cents per kilowatt-hour.	Estimated ratio of electricity costs to total miner income.

If Bitcoin Was A Country

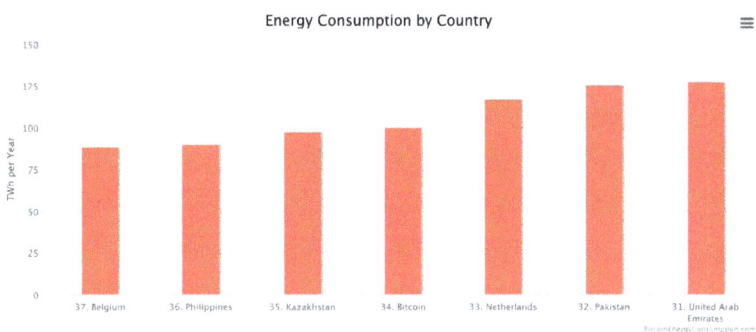

Source: bitcoinenergyconsumption.com

If Bitcoin were a country, it would rank 34th in terms of energy consumption.

Trend of Energy Consumption

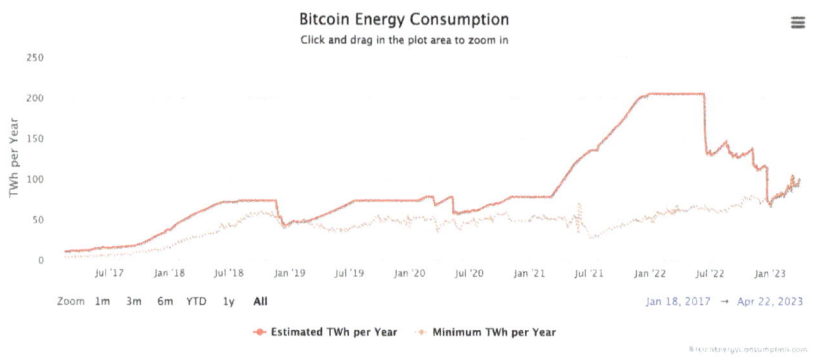

Source: bitcoinenergyconsumption.com

The trend of energy consumption is positively incremental for bitcoin network.

Can Bitcoin Move to PoS?

- Within 2140: ??
- After 2140: ??
- PoS will move the power to the 'richest in the room' while PoW gives power to the "hard worker in the room".

Brighter Sides

- 40% - 70% Renewable Energy usage
- New BTC issuance decay over time and is finite. 92% of coins are already mined. Only 15% of revenue accounts for processing transaction.
- Possibility of Global Monetary System Backed By Energy (not out of thin air)

> **Activity**

Choose the correct answer below.

1. How is the energy usage of Bitcoin mining typically measured?

   ☐ By the amount of electricity used in mining
   ☐ By the number of Bitcoin transactions processed
   ☐ By the number of Bitcoin wallets created
   ☐ By the market value of Bitcoin

2. What percentage of the world's total electricity consumption is estimated to be used for Bitcoin mining?

   ☐ Less than 0.1%   ☐ Approximately 1%   ☐ Around 5%   ☐ More than 10%

3. What is the relationship between energy usage and profitability in Bitcoin mining?

   ☐ Higher energy usage leads to higher profitability
   ☐ Higher energy usage leads to lower profitability
   ☐ Energy usage does not affect profitability
   ☐ Profitability is solely determined by the market value of Bitcoin

4. What is the primary source of energy used in Bitcoin mining?

   ☐ Renewable energy
   ☐ Fossil fuels
   ☐ Nuclear energy
   ☐ Hydroelectric power

5. Which country has the highest percentage of Bitcoin mining operations powered by renewable energy?

   ☐ China   ☐ United States   ☐ Sweden   ☐ Iceland

Activity

6. How does Bitcoin mining impact the environment in terms of carbon emissions?

   ☐ It reduces carbon emissions
   ☐ It has no impact on carbon emissions
   ☐ It contributes to increased carbon emissions
   ☐ It relies solely on renewable energy sources for mining

7. What is the estimated annual energy consumption of Bitcoin mining as of 2023?

   ☐ 0-25 TeraWatt-hours (TWh)
   ☐ 25-50 TeraWatt-hours (TWh)
   ☐ 50-100 TeraWatt-hours (TWh)
   ☐ 100-200 TeraWatt-hours (TWh)

8. If Bitcoin were a country, what would be the position of Bitcoin in the world in terms of energy usage (2023)?

   ☐ 10th   ☐ 34th   ☐ 98th   ☐ 157th

9. What is the primary factor influencing the energy usage of Bitcoin mining?

   ☐ Computational power required for mining
   ☐ Renewable energy sources used for mining
   ☐ Minimal energy requirements
   ☐ Absence of any energy consumption

Activity

10. What is the main concern raised by critics regarding the energy usage of Bitcoin mining?
    - [ ] It has no impact on the environment
    - [ ] It is powered solely by renewable energy
    - [ ] It does not require any energy
    - [ ] It contributes to environmental degradation and increased carbon emissions

Chapter 18

Noises of Altcoins

Flash Back To The Origins

Satoshi said,

> The root problem with conventional currency is all the trust that's required to make it work. The central bank must be trusted not to debase the currency, but the history of fiat currencies is full of breaches of that trust

And Bitcoin was born!

The Pandora's box of blockchain, crypto, web3 – all started with this.

Ideal Financial World

- Access to everyone, but no control to anyone
- Transparent financial structure
- Store of value; no one can debase or rebase
- Faster, easy, and cheap transactions
- Settled in real time irrespective of transaction value size.
- Time tested, portable, and acceptable everywhere
- Absolute control through ownership

There Is No Second Best

- Bitcoin has:

✘ No CEO
✘ No organization,
✘ No pre-mine
✘ No allocation to anyone
✘ No hard fork nor any hack
✘ No change on core economics
✘ No governance voting.

- All other projects compromise on decentralization or security.

There has never been a more secure, scarce, immutable, portable, and decentralized asset in our history.

Let's Verify

	Gold	Bitcoin	Altcoins
Bearer Asset	✓	✓	✓
Scarcity	✓	✓	✘
Decentralized	✓	✓	✘
Portability	✘	✓	✓
Divisibility	✘	✓	✓
Storage counter-party	✘	✓	✓
Censorship resistant	✘	✓	✓
Auditable & Predictable	✘	✓	✘

What The Fuss of Altcoins

- People wanted to control bitcoin; when they couldn't, they copied bitcoin and changes tidbits to delude newcomers in search of "next Bitcoin".
- The very second best "Ethereum" has a CEO figure "Vitalik", pre-mined 70%, hard forked because of 2016 hack, switched from PoW to PoS, with no fixed supply.
- Other altcoins are much more problematic and centralized.
- Altcoin projects narrate faster and cheaper transactions, decentralized of this and that - by allocating & creating money for themselves.

Bitcoin Maximalists vs Altcoiners

Bitcoin Maximalists	Altcoiners
- Support Bitcoin as the only cryptocurrency. - Believe Bitcoin has superior qualities such as decentralization, security, and scarcity - View Bitcoin as the only true digital gold and the best store of value - Skeptical of altcoins as unnecessary and inferior copies of Bitcoin - Focus on Bitcoin as a hedge against traditional financial systems - Skeptical of risks and complexities associated with altcoins	- Support cryptocurrencies other than Bitcoin (altcoins) - Argue that altcoins offer unique features and use cases - Diversify investments across a range of cryptocurrencies, including altcoins - Willing to take risks and explore new investment opportunities in emerging cryptocurrencies - See altcoins as potential solutions for specific use cases - See altcoins as a way to maximize profits in a dynamic market

Noises of Altcoins

Noises on Music

- There is a greater good to stay as "Bitcoin Maximalist" to achieve financial freedom, to bank the unbanked and to build a global open monetary system accessible to all.
- Except Bitcoin, all other projects are more like a gamble, experimental.
- Experiments on altcoins will serve as testnet for Bitcoin. In the future, many good features can be implemented on Bitcoin after thoroughly experimented with altcoins.
- **Altcoins are the noises - Bitcoin is the music.**

Activity

Choose the correct answer below.

1. Which of the following is a key difference between Bitcoin and altcoins?
   - [ ] Bitcoin is the only cryptocurrency, altcoins are not real cryptocurrencies
   - [ ] Bitcoin has the highest market value, altcoins are trailing in market value.
   - [ ] Bitcoin is a centralized digital currency, altcoins are decentralized
   - [ ] Bitcoin has faster transaction speed compared to altcoins.

2. What is the main difference between Bitcoin and Ethereum in terms of their monetary policies?
   - [ ] Bitcoin has a fixed supply, Ethereum has an unlimited supply
   - [ ] Bitcoin has a deflationary supply, Ethereum has an inflationary supply
   - [ ] Bitcoin has a variable supply, Ethereum has a fixed supply
   - [ ] Bitcoin and Ethereum have the same monetary policy.

3. Which of the following is considered as a commodity?
   - [ ] Bitcoin
   - [ ] Ethereum
   - [ ] Ripple
   - [ ] Litecoin.

4. How many VCs invested Satoshi in 2009 to launch Bitcoin?
   - [ ] 2
   - [ ] 0
   - [ ] 5
   - [ ] 4

5. Which of the following has higher TPS (transaction per second)?
   - [ ] Lightning Network of Bitcoin
   - [ ] Polygon of Ethereum
   - [ ] Solana
   - [ ] Aptos

Activity

6. What is the main technology difference between Bitcoin and many altcoins like Ethereum?

   ☐ Bitcoin uses proof-of-work (PoW) consensus algorithm, while altcoins use proof-of-stake (PoS)
   ☐ Bitcoin has better smart contract functionality than altcoins
   ☐ Bitcoin transactions are not transparent, while altcoin transactions are transparent
   ☐ None of the above.

7. What is the main advantage of Bitcoin over altcoins in terms of adoption and recognition?

   ☐ Bitcoin is widely accepted as commodity
   ☐ Altcoins are securities compared to Bitcoin
   ☐ Bitcoin has lower transaction fees compared to altcoins
   ☐ Altcoins have faster transaction confirmation time compared to Bitcoin.

8. Which of the following is a potential disadvantage of altcoins compared to Bitcoin?

   ☐ Higher regulatory scrutiny
   ☐ Lower liquidity
   ☐ Higher volatility
   ☐ All of the above

9. Which of the following is a key difference between Bitcoin and Ethereum?

   ☐ Ethereum has a higher market value compared to Bitcoin
   ☐ Bitcoin has faster transaction speed compared to Ethereum
   ☐ Bitcoin is a digital currency, Ethereum is a blockchain platform
   ☐ Bitcoin has smart contract functionality, while Ethereum does not.

Activity

10. Which of the following has the highest level of adoption and usage among cryptocurrencies?

    ☐ Bitcoin ☐ Ethereum ☐ Ripple ☐ Litecoin

Chapter 19: DeFi and dApps on Bitcoin

Decentralized Web Era

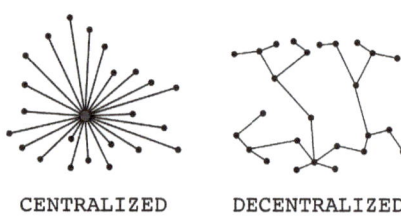

CENTRALIZED   DECENTRALIZED

- The start of internet also started the open source, decentralized, privacy focused movement.
- But most of the software and web services are built and managed by companies for data mining, ads driven motives with controlled & filtered access.
- The first successful decentralized network on finance with no central authority is Bitcoin Network.

Bitcoin drives the development of decentralized network on other domains – when connected with each other establishes a decentralized web era.

Built On Bitcoin

- Bitcoin is the first money app built on Bitcoin Network:
- Lightning Network
- Liquid Network by Blockstream
- HodlHodl p2p platform
- Sidechains like Stacks
- Ordinals, BRC-20, ORC-20, SRC-20, Inscriptions
- NOSTR supporting Bitcoin

Completely decentralized protocol based application interacting with each other.

Good Things Take Time

- Changes and upgrades to make Bitcoin more than digital assets come through BIPs (Bitcoin Improvement Proposals).
- BIPs go through audits, discussions, network participant's signals
- Lengthy journey, but Bitcoin can eventually have smart contract capabilities, NFTs, and more.

99% Decentralized = 100% Centralized

Bitcoin is 100% Decentralized.

Possibility of Decentralized Web Era can only be imagined on Bitcoin Network.

Why can't we have Decentralized Web Era with altcoins?

- The second best Ethereum is centralized with unpredictable economics.
- Building decentralized apps on even 99% centralized platforms is stupid.

That's why 99.99% Decentralized means 100% Centralized.

Link to Explore
- https://lightning.network/
- https://www.stacks.co/
- https://bisq.network/
- https://blockstream.com/
- https://ordinals.com/

> **Activity**

Choose the correct answer below.

1. Which of the following statements is true about DeFi (Decentralized Finance) and Dapps (Decentralized Applications) on Bitcoin?

    ☐ DeFi and Dapps are exclusively built on the Bitcoin blockchain
    ☐ DeFi and Dapps are not possible on the Bitcoin blockchain
    ☐ DeFi and Dapps can be built on the Bitcoin blockchain using second-layer solutions
    ☐ DeFi and Dapps can only be built on altcoins, not on Bitcoin.

2. Which of the following is a major advantage of building Dapps on the Bitcoin blockchain?

    ☐ Higher transaction speed compared to other blockchains
    ☐ Lower transaction fees compared to other blockchains
    ☐ Wider user adoption and recognition for 100% decentralization compared to other blockchains
    ☐ Advanced smart contract functionality compared to other blockchains.

3. What is the main challenge in developing DeFi and Dapps on the Bitcoin blockchain?

    ☐ Lack of scalability and transaction speed
    ☐ Limited smart contract functionality
    ☐ High transaction fees
    ☐ Lack of developer community.

4. Which of the following is an example of a DeFi protocol that operates on the Bitcoin blockchain?

    ☐ Uniswap ☐ MakerDAO ☐ Compound ☐ Atomic Finance.

> **Activity**

5. Which of the following technologies was introduced that made NFTs easy to inscribe in Bitcoin?
   - [ ] Taproot
   - [ ] Segregated Witness (SegWit)
   - [ ] Proof-of-Stake (PoS)
   - [ ] Segregated Transaction (SegTx)

6. What is the main benefit of using Segregated Witness (SegWit) in Bitcoin?
   - [ ] Increased transaction speed
   - [ ] Lower transaction fees
   - [ ] Enhanced security and privacy
   - [ ] More advanced smart contract functionality.

7. What are Ordinals in the context of Bitcoin?
   - [ ] A type of consensus algorithm
   - [ ] A privacy-enhancing feature
   - [ ] A smart contract scripting language
   - [ ] Digital artifacts inscribed on Bitcoin.

8. What are sidechains in the context of Bitcoin?
   - [ ] Additional layers on top of the Bitcoin blockchain
   - [ ] Alternative blockchains that run in parallel with the main Bitcoin blockchain
   - [ ] A type of consensus algorithm used in Bitcoin
   - [ ] Bitcoin mining operators

9. Which of the following is an example of a sidechain on Bitcoin?
   - [ ] Ethereum
   - [ ] Litecoin
   - [ ] Liquid
   - [ ] Ripple.

DeFi and dApps on Bitcoin

> Activity

10. What is the role of Bitcoin's OP_RETURN opcode in Dapps on the Bitcoin blockchain?

    - [ ] To enable faster and more scalable transactions
    - [ ] To ensure the same consensus algorithm as the main Bitcoin blockchain
    - [ ] To store data on the Bitcoin blockchain for Dapp functionality
    - [ ] To maintain a fixed exchange rate between the Dapp and the main Bitcoin blockchain.

Chapter 20 — Bitcoinization

Bitcoin As Global Money

Flaws of traditional fiat currencies:

- Inflation
- Central bank manipulation
- Lack of transparency "makes" People exit From Fiat

- Bitcoin as hard capped programmable money = Best form of "medium of exchange" + Store of Value
- Bitcoin becomes dominant global currency, Bitcoinization occurs, Bitcoin Standard sets up & Hyperbitcoinization happens.

Replacing Fiat

To use Bitcoin in everyday life by everyone:

- Bitcoin Upgrades as a form of payment by businesses and individuals.
- Distrust in traditional financial systems and fiat currencies.
- Geopolitical and economic uncertainties

Is 21m bitcoins enough?

There are 21 m BTC = 21,000,000 * 100,000,000 Sats. Just like how golds are traded in ounces or tolas, Bitcoins will be traded in Sats. If needed, decimals can be upgraded for new units.

1 BTC = 1 BTC

- Inflection point for 1 BTC = 1 BTC can be violent in price chart (but short one) where all users rush to convert their fiats to BTC.
- After inflection point, no one will accept fiats to exchange their Bitcoins. Fiats = No value
- Bitcoinization = Everything will be marked in BTC.
- BTC value will not get displayed in fiats like USD, Euro, NPR
- **This is called Bitcoin Standard.**

Light In the Chaos

There are two precursors for Bitcoinization to happen:

1. People became aware of Bitcoin. Slower & Smooth Transition
2. Financial Collapse. Abrupt & Dangerous Transition

Bitcoin is an exit door. Bitcoin is a light in the time of financial chaos. Country Leaders should understand & direct this transition in time.

The Good, The Bad and The Ugly

Good:

- Financial inclusivity, especially for the unbanked populations.
- Lower fees and faster cross-border transactions.
- Reduction of corruption and illicit activities through transparency.
- Protection against inflation and potential preservation of wealth with SoV.

Bad:

- Volatility with price fluctuations.
- Regulatory and legal challenges.
- Lack of consumer protections and potential for scams and fraud.

Ugly:

- Governmental crackdowns, & bans
- CBDC wars
- Global wealth collapse

That's Why It's Only Bitcoin

- Fiats' days are numbered.
- There is no second best to Bitcoin
- Human civilization is driven by "fights" for freedom.
- Bitcoin is our path for financial freedom.
- That's why it's only Bitcoin that matters.

Activity

Choose the correct answer below.

1. What is "Bitcoinization"?

    ☐ The process of converting Bitcoin into other cryptocurrencies
    ☐ The widespread adoption of Bitcoin as a legal tender or currency
    ☐ A term used to describe the decline of Bitcoin's value
    ☐ The process of mining new Bitcoins.

2. Which country has adopted Bitcoin as legal tender in 2021?

    ☐ United States ☐ El Salvador ☐ China ☐ Japan.

3. What is the main advantage of Bitcoinization for a country's economy?

    ☐ Increased financial inclusion
    ☐ Decreased volatility of the national currency
    ☐ Lower transaction fees
    ☐ Enhanced privacy and security.

4. How does Bitcoinization affect the traditional banking system in a country?

    ☐ It strengthens the traditional banking system
    ☐ It weakens the traditional banking system
    ☐ It has no impact on the traditional banking system
    ☐ It replaces the traditional banking system.

5. What is not the potential benefit of the bitcoin standard for individuals?

    ☐ Protection against inflation
    ☐ Increased financial privacy
    ☐ Higher transaction fees
    ☐ Efficient taxation.

Activity

6. How does Bitcoinization affect the government's control over the economy?

   ☐ It increases the government's control over the economy
   ☐ It decreases the government's control over the economy
   ☐ It has no impact on the government's control over the economy
   ☐ It eliminates the need for government control over the economy.

7. What are the potential risks associated with Bitcoinization?

   ☐ Increased risk of fraud and scams
   ☐ Higher market volatility
   ☐ Lack of consumer protection
   ☐ All of the above.

8. What is the role of regulation in Bitcoinization?

   ☐ Regulation is necessary to ensure safe and legal use of Bitcoin
   ☐ Regulation is not needed for Bitcoinization
   ☐ Regulation hinders the adoption of Bitcoin
   ☐ Regulation promotes illegal use of Bitcoin.

9. What is "bitcoin standard"?

   ☐ A globally accepted standard for Bitcoin wallets
   ☐ A fixed exchange rate between Bitcoin and other cryptocurrencies
   ☐ A monetary system where Bitcoin serves as the base currency
   ☐ A set of rules and regulations governing Bitcoin transactions

> **Activity**

10. What are the factors that can influence the success of Bitcoinization in a country?
    - ☐ Government support and regulation
    - ☐ Financial infrastructure and technological readiness
    - ☐ Public acceptance and adoption
    - ☐ All of the above.

Chapter 21 — Into The Bitcoin Lingo

Crypto Lingo	Definition
HODL	A slang for the word Hold, as in 'Hold on to your bitcoins, do not sell!'
Rekt	Complete loss of money with no hope of recovery
FOMO	Short form for "Fear Of Missing Out"
FUD	Stands for Fear, Uncertainty, and Doubt
WAGMI	We All Gonna Make it
WAGMIA	We All Gonna Make It Again
NGMI	Never/Not Gonna Make It
NGU	Number Go Up
Whale	Anyone holding a large number of tokens of any crypto
Rugpull	Common exit scam where the developers of a Web3 startup announce a project and attract external investors, only to run with the money and abandon the project

Crypto Lingo	Definition
Mooning	Seeing a big spike or expected to spike (going to the moon)
ICO	Initial Coin Offering: A common way for crypto projects to raise money for their business
ATH	All-Time High
Bag Holder	Anyone with crypto not selling when in profit then watching price fall down
Buy the dip	Opportunity to accumulate crypto at lower prices
DeFi	Decentralized finance
DEX	Decentralized Exchange
Smart contracts	Self-executing digital contracts that allow some form of direct exchange between two people
Public key	The keys which you need to receive crypto
Private key	The keys which you need to send/spend crypto
Wallet	Application that you need to manage your private/public keys
PoW	Proof-of-Work
PoS	Proof-of-Stake
DCA	Dollar Cost Average: A reliable strategy which involves buying fixed amounts of crypto at regular intervals instead of trying to time your entry into the market

Crypto Lingo	Definition
Long Position	A 'long' is a type of trade where you can turn a profit by betting that an asset will increase in value.
Short Position	A 'short' is a type of trade where you can turn a profit by betting that an asset will decrease in value.
Altcoin	All crypto coins except Bitcoin.
Volatility	Price fluctuations.
ROI	Return on Investment.
Market Cap	The total circulating supply of coins multiplied by the price of each coin.
Fiat	Any currency backed by a government or country (USD, AUD, Euro, etc).
Bull Market or Bullish	Upward trend in the market; price increase.
Bear Market or Bearish	Downward trend in the market; price decrease.
SATS	Smallest unit of Bitcoin; 0.00000001 BTC. (Or 100 million Sats = 1 BTC).
NFTs	Non-fungible Tokens.
Good Morning	Cryptocurrency based on a joke.
Pump & Dump	Artificially inflate prices & get people to invest before big holders conspire to sell all at once, leaving naive investors empty-handed
White Paper	A document on a particular crypto coin, underlining its utility, purpose, future prospects & underlying technology

Crypto Lingo	Definition
Arbitrage	Buying cryptocurrency on one exchange and selling it for a higher price on another exchange.
Stablecoin	Cryptocurrency that is pegged to a stable asset (e.g., U.S. Dollar).
Shitcoin	A worthless and dead coin with no real value.
Lambo	Cryptocurrency reaches a value high enough to buy yourself a Lamborghini.
CT	Crypto Twitter.
DYOR	Do Your Own Research.
JOMO	Joy Of Missing Out.
Mixer	Software that makes bitcoin transactions anonymous and untraceable.
Flippening	An event where a cryptocurrency (altcoin) surpasses another coin/project in market capitalization.
Fork	Blockchain splits into another separate chain.
FUDster	Anyone who is intentionally spreading FUD (Fear, Uncertainty, and Doubt) about cryptocurrency.
Genesis Block	The first block to be mined in a blockchain.
Mining	Solving complex math problems in order to create cryptocurrency & ensure the Blockchain network & its transactions are kept verified & secure
Altseason	A brief period where money flows out of Bitcoin & into altcoins, resulting in a significant & rapid price increase for the majority of cryptocurrencies.

Crypto Lingo	Definition
SAFU	Secure Asset Fund for Users.
AMM	Automated Market Maker.
BTFD	Buy The Fucking Dip, a slang term used to encourage buying a cryptocurrency when its price is low.
DLT	Distributed Ledger Technology.
Dust	A small amount of cryptocurrency that remains in a user wallet after a transaction, usually of very low value.
Liquidity	Value backing the crypto assets for efficient market making.
UTXO	Unspent Transaction Output.
Whitelist	A list of approved addresses allowed to participate in a particular cryptocurrency network.
P2P	Peer to Peer.
Multi-Sig	Requires more than one signature to authorize a transaction.
KYC	Know Your Customer. KYC is a process that requires companies to verify the identity of their customers.
Hash	A cryptographic function that takes an input of any size and produces an output of a fixed size.
Shill	Someone purposely promoting a coin or project for their own benefit - they usually hold the asset they are 'shilling'.
Faucet	Reward system on a website or app that offers free cryptocurrency for signing up or completing certain tasks.

Crypto Lingo	Definition
Gas Price or Mining Fee	Amount paid to miners or validators for verifying and executing transactions on the network.
EVM	Ethereum Virtual Machine (EVM) is a virtual machine contained in every node on the Ethereum network.
Double Spend	A potential process that allows someone to spend the same cryptocurrency more than once.
Signature	A type of cryptographic signature that is used to verify the authenticity of a transaction or message.
Cold Storage	A process of storing the seed phrase or master key offline on a device that is not connected to the internet.
Burned	Coins are removed from circulation
AML	Anti-Money Laundering
Airdrop	Distributing new tokens to the cryptocurrency community
51% Attack	Single entity or group gaining control of over 50% of mining power
Oracles	Data feeds that bring off-chain data onto the blockchain for smart contracts
Turing Completeness	System or language capable of completing any calculation like a human
TOR	Software that protects users' privacy when surfing the internet
ERC-20	Ethereum Request for Comments: protocol used to standardize the development of Ethereum-based applications.
DAO	Decentralized Autonomous Organization

Crypto Lingo	Definition
dApp	Decentralized application
Consensus	Agreement of all network nodes on transaction validity
Bitcoin Maximalist	Someone who believes that Bitcoin is the only valuable cryptocurrency
Diamond Hands	Strong risk appetite of holder
Paper Hands	Weak risk appetite of holder
LFG	Expression of excitement or enthusiasm
Vaporware	Blockchain or software project that is still a concept
Normie	Person with a traditional mindset and little knowledge of cryptocurrencies
CBDC	Central Bank's Digital Currencies
IYKYK	Expression used for insider knowledge
Degens	People who buy assets expecting others to speculate on price swings
Cryptosis	Someone who strives to absorb every bit of information about crypto
PoAP	Protocol that creates digital badges for proving attendance
Tokenomics	Economic model associated with a cryptocurrency token

Crypto Lingo	Definition
Zero Knowledge	Cryptography that allows proving knowledge without revealing information
Seed Phrase	Series of words used to access a wallet in case of loss
CeFi	Centralized finance
Testnet	Testing environment for blockchain
Mainnet	Actual stable network of blockchain
On-chain	Refers to transactions recorded on the blockchain
BUIDL	Slang for "Build"
Ape	Practice of investing in a cryptocurrency token shortly after its launch without researching the project thoroughly
CTO	Community Takeover

21 Myths & Misconceptions About Bitcoin

1. Bitcoin is another digital payment system like PayPal or Online Banking.
2. Bitcoin is controlled by core developers.
3. Miners can change the bitcoin rules with 51% attack.
4. Bitcoin has voting governance system through 1-CPU-1-Vote.
5. Bitcoin value is backed by electricity & computation power.
6. Bitcoin is worthless since it is not backed by anything.
7. Early adopters of bitcoin are unfairly rewarded higher.
8. 21 million bitcoins isn't enough for 8 billion population.
9. Bitcoin is stored in wallets.
10. Bitcoin is a pyramid or Ponzi scheme.
11. Bitcoin will suffer deflationary death spiral.
12. Bitcoin will fail in real world since there is no CEO or Organization to manage it.
13. After 21 million coins are mined, no one will generate new blocks without block rewards.
14. Quantum computers would break Bitcoin's security.
15. Government will shut down bitcoin operation.
16. Bitcoin mining is a waste of energy and harmful for environment.
17. Bitcoin is only for criminals, terrorists and money launderers.
18. Bitcoin was hacked.
19. People will eventually lose all bitcoins.
20. Bitcoin helps to evade taxes and hide money.
21. Bitcoin is slow, and unscalable to handle real world transactions.

Activity: Answers

Chapter 1: Magic of Money

1)b 2)d 3)c 4)a 5)b 6)c 7)b 8)a 9)c 10)d

Chapter 2: Finding Satoshi Nakomoto

1)b 2)a 3)a 4)a 5)a 6)b 7)d 8)a 9)d 10)c 11)c

Chapter 3: Capping the World at 21 Million

1)b 2)d 3)a 4)a 5)a 6)b 7)b 8)b 9)d 10)a

Chapter 4: Halving Supply Shock

1)c 2)c 3)b 4)b 5)a 6)c 7)a 8)b 9)d 10)b

Chapter 5: Proof of work vs Out of thin air

1)c 2)b 3)a 4)d 5)d 6)c 7)b 8)a 9)b 10)c

Chapter 6: Becoming a Node. Verify, Don't Trust

1)b 2)d 3)c 4)b 5)a 6)a 7)d 8)d 9)d 10)b

Chapter 7: Civil War of 2017

1)a 2)a 3)a 4)a 5)d 6)d 7)a 8)d 9)d 10)c

Chapter 8: Break Me (Bitcoin) if You Can

1)a 2)a 3)c 4)d 5)a 6)a 7)a 8)a 9)a 10)d
11)d 12)d 13)d 14)b 15)d

Chapter 9: Scaling into the future

1)a 2)c 3)b 4)d 5)a 6)d 7)b 8)c 9)b 10)a 11)c

Chapter 10: How to Acquire Bitcoin

1)a 2)c 3)b 4)d 5)a 6)b 7)d 8)a 9)c 10)a

Chapter 11: Price of 1 Bitcoin

1)a 2)a 3)b 4)a 5)b 6)c 7)d 8)a 9)d 10)a

Chapter 12: Wallets vs Banks

1)b 2)c 3)c 4)c 5)a 6)b 7)b 8)b 9)d 10)a

Chapter 13: Apolitical Manifesto

1)b 2)d 3)b 4)a 5)a 6)c 7)a 8)a 9)b 10)d

Chapter 14: Financial Freedom

1)a 2)c 3)d 4)a 5)d 6)b 7)a 8)a 9)d 10)c

Chapter 15: Inheritance Planning

1)a 2)c 3)d 4)c 5)c 6)a 7)d 8)b 9)b 10)a

Chapter 16: Global Adoption vs Global Banning

1)c 2)c 3)a 4)a 5)d 6)a 7)d 8)d 9)d 10)c

Chapter 17: Energy Debate

1)a 2)a 3)b 4)a 5)d 6)c 7)d 8)b 9)a 10)d

Chapter 18: Noises of Altcoins

1)b 2)a 3)a 4)b 5)a 6)d 7)a 8)d 9)c 10)a

Chapter 19: DeFi and dApps on Bitcoin

1)c 2)c 3)b 4)d 5)a 6)b 7)d 8)b 9)c 10)c

Chapter 20: Bitcoinization

1)b 2)b 3)a 4)b 5)c 6)b 7)d 8)a 9)c 10)d

www.ingramcontent.com/pod-product-compliance
Lightning Source LLC
Chambersburg PA
CBHW052258220526
45471CB00001B/399